S0-AKQ-514

PIONEERS & POLITICIANS

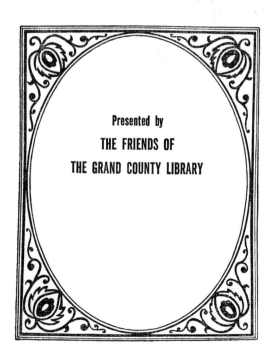

Presented by

**THE FRIENDS OF
THE GRAND COUNTY LIBRARY**

For Dottie and Gay

PIONEERS & POLITICIANS

10 Colorado Governors in Profile

Richard D. Lamm and Duane A. Smith

PRUETT **P** PUBLISHING COMPANY
Boulder, Colorado

Library of Congress Cataloging in Publication Data

Lamm, Richard D.
  Pioneers and politicians.

  Bibliography: p.
  Includes index.
  1. Colorado—Governors—Biography. 2. Colorado—
Politics and government. I. Smith, Duane A. II. Title.
III. Title: Pioneers and politicians.
F775.L36 1984   978.8'009'92 (B)   84-18380
ISBN 0-87108-670-0 (pbk.)

First Edition
1 2 3 4 5 6 7 8 9

Printed in the United States of America

Contents

Preface

Determined and dilatory, successful and unsuccessful, lucky and unlucky—the roll of Colorado governors covers a period nearly twice the biblical three score and ten of a man's life span. And men they have all been (Colorado has yet to honor any of its qualified women with the office). They represent the best and the worst, and much in between, of what we call Colorado's heritage. The difference between them and other Coloradans is only that they secured an appointment or won an election that attached the term governor to their names for a specified term and a lifetime thereafter.

For many people who pick up this volume, the names will be unfamiliar or only a vague echo of a school day's memory, which is unfortunate and testifies to a parochialism that plagues this generation. Some of these men were long ago relegated to the mine dump of Colorado history, to be picked over by historians and antiquarians in their quiet search to rediscover the past. There they have weathered the years and endured their generation's fading and disappearance.

When we undertook this project several years ago, our plan was to select governors from the nineteenth and twentieth centuries to portray the office and the diversity of individuals who held it. Our goal was to write short biographies, anticipating that they would whet the reader's appetite for pursuing the story further. As Ralph Waldo Emerson wrote over a century ago, "There is properly no history; only biography." These biographies are not definitive; that task we leave to future writers. The raw material is there, awaiting discovery by Colorado's James Boswell.

We had another objective in mind. Historian Edmund S. Morgan expressed it well when he wrote in 1983: "History, like other forms of literature, may reach its highest function in furnishing vicarious experience, in enabling us to escape from the parochialism of the present to the larger world of the past." Colorado's engaging past makes fictionalizing it unnecessary; the only problem for the historian is to unlock its secrets and make it come alive on the printed page.

As in any project of this nature, we owe unpayable debts of gratitude to the host of people whose kindness and professionalism helped make this book possible: the staffs of the Colorado Historical Society, Western Historical Collections, University of Colorado, Fort Lewis College Library, Colorado State Archives, Amon Carter Museum, and Western History Department, Denver Public Library. Katherine Kane, Catherine Conrad, Janette Crandall, Collette Chambellan, Kathy Richardson, Tom Noel, George DeLuca, Eleanor Gehres, and Barbara Sudler performed a variety of tasks, including typing and researching to reading manuscript chapters. Bill Hosokawa, John Love, Stephen McNichols, Gene Breitenstein, and Ben Poxson generously contributed their time and memories in interviews. Our thanks also to Jerry Keenan, Merilee Eggleston, and the helpful staff at Pruett Publishing.

Writers do not live and work in an impersonal void—they need the encouragement, support, and, in a real sense, the sacrifice of their families. We gratefully acknowledge our indebtedness to them and dedicate this book to our wives with the sentiment of Robert Browning, who, upon completing a volume of poetry, wrote to his wife: "*Take them, Love, the book and me together: Where the heart lies, let the brain lie also.*"

Introduction: The Colorado Governorship

Thirty-four men have been governor of Colorado since it became a state on August 1, 1876 (seven during the territorial years). They have held the office for periods of time varying from nine days to ten-and-a-half years. Seventeen have been Republicans and sixteen have been Democrats; one, Davis H. Waite, was a Populist. Of the forty-eight elections, starting with 1876, the Democrats have won twenty-four, the Republicans twenty-two, and the Populists one. The election of 1904 ended in chaos and confusion. Alva Adams' victory was contested and led eventually to the seating of the Republican, under conditions that made it difficult to declare a real winner. In the first 108 years of statehood, Democrats have held the governorship 53 years, Republicans 53 years, and the Populists 2.

All Colorado governors have been white males, mostly Protestant. For forty-one elections, governors have served two-year terms; for seven elections, since 1958, they have served four-year terms. Colorado was one of the last states to shift to the longer term and only four states, in 1984, retained a two-year term.

The governor's salary has gone steadily upward, particularly in the past quarter of a century. In 1876 he made $3,000; in 1900, $5,000; in 1930, $5,000; in 1960, $20,000; in 1972, $40,000; in 1982, $60,000. Interestingly, of the 50,000 state employees, the governor appoints only his cabinet (15 people) and personal staff.

Not until Teller Ammons in 1937 did the first native-born governor take office. Up to that time Ohio had contributed six men (seven, if Robert Steele, governor of the short-lived Jefferson Territory is counted) and Illinois four. The majority have come from the Midwest, reflecting Colorado's overall population pattern. The favorite birth months for Colorado's governors have been January, August, November, and December, which produced a total of nineteen. April and June gave the state six more, leaving long odds against election of anyone born in the other six months.

Although their careers varied considerably, they were generally a predictable group of ambitious, but not obsessed, politicians. Of the thirty-four men, only three went on to Washington, D.C., three as senators (C. Thomas, J. Shafroth, E. Johnson) and one as congressman (Shafroth). Their occupations varied—smelterman, miner, newspaperman, minister, businessman, farmer. As might be expected, mining, ranching, business, and law dominated the nineteenth century. Some were wealthy, most middle class. As far as we know, they were honest men, with only one, Clarence Morley, being convicted of a felony after he left office.

Colorado's political history shows clearly that it is a swing state. For example, there was a period of Republican dominance from 1876 to 1909, when ten Republicans, one Democrat, and two Populists served in the House of Representatives, eight serving more than one term and two changing parties along the way. The Democrats dominated the Republicans seven to one from 1910 to 1918. In the years from 1918 to 1966 ten Republicans and thirteen Democrats represented Colorado, only four as one-termers. Since 1966 the Democrats have held a slight edge, seven to six. From 1876 through 1980 Colorado gave a plurality of its votes to seventeen Republican presidential candidates and ten Democrats.

The challenges faced by Colorado's chief executives and the demands of the job have differed with the times. Territorial Governor William Gilpin spent three months of a year's appointment in Washington (two of them defending his administration), and John Evans left Colorado for months on end to lobby in the East. John Routt, while governor, purchased and worked the Morning Star mine at Leadville. Governor Henry Buchtel ran both the state and the University of Denver—an arduous but manageable task. Billy Adams campaigned very little in his three winning races, never spending over $5,000 nor giving many speeches.

Recent Colorado governors might envy what appears to be their predecessors' less pressure-filled roles. Those men, on the other hand, would probably have considered themselves to be as busy as their successors, even though the legislature met only every other year. The pace of politics was undoubtedly less hectic in those years when judged by 1984 standards. Part of this difference reflects subtle changes in the perception of the governor's role, the state's economy, and the communications revolution.

Colorado's economic history may be roughly divided into three eras. The first third is devoted mainly to mining, the second third mostly to agriculture. Starting during World War II with the arrival of numerous federal facilities and accelerating in the postwar era, Colorado's economy and population exploded, giving governors new and different challenges. Between 1860 and 1960 Colorado's population increased fiftyfold, while the United States' population grew sixfold. Providing the water and educational facilities for a fast-growing and diverse state has always been a challenge, one which has grown in proportion to the population. Colorado's manufacturing work force grew from 74,000 jobs in 1958 to 182,000 in 1982.

Some problems never change. Water, for instance, has been a source of conflict and controversy ever since Colorado became a state; every Colorado governor has dealt to some degree with the problem of water.

Other challenges came with the times. Governor Steve McNichols's history-making advances in the mental health field and the explosion of higher education under John Love would have caused earlier governors to shake their heads in disbelief. Surprisingly, Colorado has always been a somewhat urban state with more than fifty percent of its population, in recent years, in the Denver metropolitan

3

area. However, only in later years have governors and legislatures been forced to wrestle with "urban problems" as we know them today. John Love personally helped quell a riot in Denver the night Martin Luther King was assassinated. Colorado governors have often been caught in the conflict between urban and rural communities and between city and suburb. Prior to the court-ordered reapportionment in 1964, political power in Colorado was clearly in the rural areas.

Powers of the Colorado Governor

Colorado's constitution was written during an era when a lack of trust in government prompted many more restrictions on power and the constitution. This limitation of power is not a recent development. Colorado's document, drafted in 1876, is three times longer than those of other states drafted prior to 1850. The intention of the framers was to restrict power and prevent its abuse. They succeeded brilliantly. John Love put it so well when he said, "Colorado governors have the responsibility but not the authority to run the state." Colorado clearly has what political scientists call a "weak governor system."

In 1965, a political science study ranking the appointive powers of the governor placed Colorado last of all fifty states. Even with the reorganization of 1968, which expanded Colorado's executive power to appoint, a Colorado governor can appoint only fifteen out of the twenty department heads. According to one political scientist, the Colorado constitution "seriously limits the governor's capacity to administer the affairs of the state."

Joseph A. Schlesinger, in *Politics in the American States: A Comparative Analysis* (1963), does rate Colorado high on potential powers because of the lack of limitation on the governor's tenure, a source of strength not common in other states, that allows Colorado governors to remain a political threat beyond the traditional two terms. In an overall combined index of the formal powers of the governor, Schlesinger finds Colorado to be right in the middle of the fifty states, with Colorado having a rating of fourteen with the median score of all states being thirteen.

The Colorado governor has no substantial budgetary power because a number of "earmarked funds," such as the Wildlife Fund and Highway Users Trust Fund, further limit the chief executive's powers. Most studies of Colorado state government comment on how few budgetary powers the Colorado governor has. Starting in the early 1960s, with a power struggle and personality conflict between State Senator Joe Shoemaker, chairman of the powerful Joint Budget Committee, and Governor John Love, the legislature asserted more and more authority over the budget and started using the budget as an indirect method of controlling the government.

In his book *Budgeting is the Answer*, Joe Shoemaker states:

> Virtually all visiting legislators and reporters from other states are struck by the startling degree of control that the Colorado Legislature retains over the state's spending. In most states, much of that power is given, at least de facto, to the governor. And this of course is the vital distinction between Colorado and the other states. For money is power and the control of money is thus the control of power, The power of government is felt most often when it redistributes wealth and reallocates resources.

One important source of control for Colorado's governor comes through the traditional veto power (subject to a two-thirds override by the legislature) and also the item veto, enabling him to veto any items in a bill "making appropriations of money."

Colorado voters have feared giving too many powers to the governor. In 1934, they overwhelmingly defeated (200,000 to 47,000) a plan that would have given the executive broad powers to reorganize the government. In 1960, another very similar amendment was defeated (430,000 to 170,000) because of the same fears—that the new powers would turn Colorado's governorship into a "dictatorship." The subtle erosions and inefficiencies engendered by the "weak governor" concept are not readily apparent in Colorado and certainly are much less feared than the "spoils system," which is the usual interpretation of strong executive powers.

The attorney general, treasurer, and secretary of state are all separately elected officers, and none of them is directly responsible to the governor. The responsibility for kindergarten through twelfth grade education is in the hands of a separately elected State Board of Education. whose chief executive officer is appointed by the board, not the governor. Higher education is administered through a series of boards and the Commission on Higher Education. The regents of the University of Colorado are separately elected and have the authority to run the university. They are not accountable to the governor. The other boards of higher education, while appointed by the governor, are the dominant managers of their respective institutions, and the governor has very little influence or control over them. A strong tradition of independence and separate responsibility prevails in all of the above-mentioned offices and boards. Colorado's governor, then, not having control of either K through 12 education or higher education in any meaningful way, has two-thirds of the budget administered by a system that he or she is all but powerless to affect.

Colorado has few patronage appointments. The highway budget, another large budgetary item, is controlled by the Highway Commission, again appointed by the governor but very independent of him. Thus another source of the chief executive's power in other states has been removed from Colorado's political process. State purchasing and contracting are done on a competitive basis, mainly through a state purchasing officer who is in the civil service system and insulated from the governor's influence and control.

Thus, though the state constitution vests the governor with the "supreme executive power of the state," such power is, in many instances, illusory, and Colorado governors often are forced to rely more on the "bully pulpit," using the media to rally public support as a substitute for direct control.

The Multiple Roles
of the Governor

CHIEF EXECUTIVE OF THE
STATE OF COLORADO

The Colorado governor is the largest employer in the State of Colorado, having over 50,000 state employees. As the manager of the executive branch, the governor appoints fifteen department heads, and recruits and appoints thousands of other people every year to boards and commissions.

LEGISLATIVE LEADER

Some Colorado governors have been powerful legislative leaders at the same time they served as governor. Steve McNichols spent considerable time on the second floor of the Colorado State Capitol, lobbying and cajoling his program through the legislature. The situation is a constantly changing mix of personalities, with certain governors and certain legislative leaders being more or less suited to this leadership style.

HEAD OF PARTY

The governor is the leader of his state political party. He is expected to, and generally does, play a role in filling party leadership positions, spends considerable time on party fundraising, recruits candidates, and otherwise gets involved in party affairs.

NATIONAL POLITICAL FIGURE

Colorado governors have played various roles at the national level. Although much of the political center of gravity in this country has moved to the national Congress, governors still play a national role in their political party, John Love and Steve McNichols serving as examples in recent years.

CEREMONIAL CHIEF

Colorado governors have always had to perform a wide variety of ceremonial functions, from ribbon cuttings and receiving petitions to signing proclamations declaring National Carrier Pigeon Week. They preside over the opening of the Colorado State Fair in Pueblo, make graduation speeches at the CLETA ceremonies (Colorado Law Enforcement Training Academy), and inevitably endure picture demands that approximate fifty a week.

HUSBAND, FATHER

While performing all of the above functions, the governor must give first priority to keeping his marriage and his family together. Juggling all of these demands does not make it easy.

How Governors Spend Their Time

Activity	Percentage of Total Working Time*
Managing state government	27 percent
Working with the legislature	18 percent
Ceremonial functions	13 percent
Working with the press & other media	7 percent
Working with federal government	7 percent
Working with local governments	7 percent
Political activities	8 percent
Recruiting and appointing	8 percent
Miscellaneous activities	9 percent

*Total does not equal 100 percent as figures are averages of the responses of estimates of the portion of a governor's worktime devoted to a particular activity.

Colorado governors have had distinctive leadership styles. Some have assumed active roles (Steve McNichols) and others reactive ("Events are in the saddle and ride mankind," said one former Colorado governor). Colorado's governors articulate their policies in a variety of ways: through a State of the State address every January, which is provided for in Colorado's constitution; through their budget message and budget documents, which are delivered early in the year; and through speeches and other special messages often sent to the legislature regarding special legislation. Despite their different styles, most Colorado governors have, at a minimum, been active day-to-day managers of state government and have broadly articulated the problems they see facing the state. Early Colorado governors spent considerable time in an economic development role, whereas later Colorado governors have spent a great deal of time controlling the effects of high growth rates. Some Colorado governors have run their department heads and some have been run by them. One governor, pointing out the limitations of Colorado's constitution, said, "You serve, you do not rule."

Colorado's first ladies have all had considerable demands made on them, but here again, different women have played the role in different ways. Some have remained largely in the background, content in the role of wife and mother; others have been activists in a variety of ways. All of Colorado's governors except William Gilpin (a bachelor) and Alexander Cummings, Samuel Elbert, Billy Adams, and Ralph Carr (widowed) were married during their years in office and their wives worked as full-time, unpaid first ladies. Their duties ranged from performing ceremonial functions and hosting social events to fighting hard for women's suffrage in the nineteenth century. Merrilynn Vanderhoof was employed outside the home by a Denver television station, and Dottie Lamm writes a column for the *Denver Post*.

In addition to the thirty or so invitations that the governor receives daily, his wife customarily receives a large number of invitations for speeches, welcoming words, and social obligations. These women, from the 1860s to the present, have had the ability to command the attention of the news media, and in their many individual ways have influenced legislators, the media, department heads, and the governors on policy decisions.

Colorado 1861-1876

In the fifteen years from the time it acquired territorial status to the day it became a state, Colorado changed more profoundly than during any other time in its history. Colorado of 1861 was barely removed from the Pike's Peak gold rush of two years before and the wilderness of the Central Rockies prior to that.

Denver, Boulder, and a few mining camps populated the area, while miner/prospectors infiltrated the mountains, occasionally crossing the Continental Divide to pan and mine. Of those tiny Western Slope settlements, only Breckenridge would become permanent. Cheyennes, Utes, and Arapahoes still roamed the land, creating uneasiness but little immediate danger.

Farming, still in its infancy, coped with uncertain growing seasons, markets, and crops untested by the vagaries of a high altitude climate. Mining was undergoing a transformation from placer diggings with their free gold to hard rock mining with its need for investment, experience, and smelters to solve the riddle of complex ores.

Log and frame architecture predominated; Denver, with 4,726 residents (1860 census), headed the list of settlements in order of population. It, like all the others, relied on wagon trains to bring in food and settlers, and on the stagecoach for mail, news, and those few immigrants who could afford the price of a ticket from the states. It was a territory with more of a future than a present; indeed, mining, its principal industry, was already showing signs of decline.

By 1876 Colorado had experienced a period of mining bust and rebirth, the staggering blow of losing population and publicity to rival mining territories, and the trauma of being bypassed by the transcontinental railroad. All that was behind it now—six railroads had come into Denver, hauling freight, settlers, mail, health seekers, and tourists with much more dependability than wagons and stages. The Denver and Rio Grande Railroad and other lines were taking the benefits of this nineteenth-century transportation wonder beyond the capital. Denver was in the process of increasing its population from the 4,759 residents of 1870 to over 35,000 ten years later. Boulder had acquired the state university and a population nearing three thousand. Mining camps were popping up like mushrooms in the high country.

Gold mining had not been abandoned, but silver now claimed the headlines of the day. Farming was spreading along the foothills and out onto the plains; the Union Colony around Greeley had particularly outstanding success with its irrigation system. The Cheyennes and Arapahoes were gone, and there were rumblings for removal of the Utes from the Western Slope to make room for settlement already taking hold in the San Juans, the Gunnison country, and elsewhere. Industry, particularly smelting, was growing in Black Hawk and Denver, and Coloradans were pushing a new business called tourism. All told, Colorado looked promising in that wonderful year of the nation's centennial, 1876.

William Gilpin. *Courtesy Colorado Historical Society.*

Success in Failure: William Gilpin

For the dust-weary passengers the six-day ride was nearly over when on May 27, 1861, the triweekly stage from St. Joseph and Leavenworth lumbered into the outskirts of a roughhewn Denver. Fortunately for the nine people crowded into the coach with the overburdened name of the Central Overland and California and Pike's Peak Express Company, the past week had been blessed with summerlike days. Even in the best of weather the constantly swaying coach exhausted its passengers, but they found some compensation in the one advantage it held over other means of reaching the gold fields—speed. Precisely at half past four, according to the *Rocky Mountain News*, the COC express reached its destination, and the two ladies and seven men alighted onto the street, their plains journey over.

Nothing unusual had occurred during the crossing. The only thing that distinguished this stage from others was the presence of bearded, lanky six-footer William Gilpin, the first territorial governor of Colorado. He could not fail to notice the changes that had come to the site since he had last visited it in 1843 as a member of John C. Fremont's second western expedition. There had been nothing then—only barren land and an uninterrupted horizon. Frame and log buildings now crowded together to form a community that already aspired to greatness.

The fascinating William Gilpin had squeezed several careers into his forty-five years. Born in Delaware, he enjoyed a childhood that reflected the status and position of his wealthy Quaker family. After graduating from the University of Pennsylvania at age seventeen, he turned from his Quaker heritage when West Point beckoned. Six months there convinced young William that he was unsuited for so regimented a life. He did not, however, completely forsake the military life, and before 1850 served in the Seminole War in Florida, the Mexican War, and the plains campaign against Indians who threatened the Santa Fe Trail. Gilpin matured into a good soldier, displaying courage and leadership in several battles.

Between military stints the future governor busied himself as a newspaper editor, a rather inept farmer, a speculator and promoter, a lawyer, and a politician. Perhaps his greatest fame arose from his career as a writer, publicist, speaker, and western "boomer." In the years before coming to Colorado Gilpin lived in destiny's gateway, Independence, Missouri. Ever restless, he practiced law, ran unsuccessfully for governor and Congress, and spoke and wrote about the unlimited future of the West.

Gilpin's *The Central Gold Region*, published in 1860, predicted that the Mississippi Valley would be the future center of civilization, with Denver as its capital. No wonder Gilpin's subsequent appointment to a young Colorado was hailed by midwesterners and Pike's Peakers, who heartily endorsed his words. The slavery controversy, which erupted in neighboring Kansas in the mid-fifties, had pushed Gilpin into the Republican party. Strong support of Abraham Lincoln in the exciting 1860 campaign opened the door to his appointment. All events converged on that May afternoon in 1861, far from Washington and Missouri. Now William Gilpin would be given an opportunity denied to many authors, the opportunity to nurture his prophecies to fruition.

The man who stepped down from that stagecoach into Colorado history was a complex individual. Certainly a dreamer and a visionary, and possibly a bit eccentric, he also fearlessly and vigorously supported what he believed in. His courage and western experience could never be questioned. He had tasted both success and failure; it is evident that he had a knack for rubbing some people the wrong way. With his friends, the governor was an entertaining companion, comfortable both in the ballroom and in the bivouac.

A great deal had happened since his first visit in 1843 to what would be Colorado territory. Gilpin was one who had forecast great mineral deposits in the Rocky Mountains, and he observed with interest and enthusiasm the glory days of 1859, when 100,000 people, give or take a few, had rushed west to stake their future on the golden vision of the Pike's Peak region. He could only have been pleased with this development. Probably only a quarter of those rushers ever actually reached the gold diggings and stayed to create permanent settlement. The rest "busted" for one reason or another, but another wave of migration came in 1860 and with it some stability. The "go-backers" had bet wrong.

Farms, ranches, and towns soon came into being to give mining the support it needed. Town platting and promotion became popular pastimes. Many of these would-be communities died at birth, but Denver thrived. Although gold discoveries on the site of Denver gave it its start, it never developed into a mining camp in the true sense of the word. From the beginning Denver flourished as a trading, business, and trans-shipment center—the gateway to the mountains. Blessed with aggressive newspapers, businessmen, and other leaders, Denver set its course to become the dominant community. Rivals fell in the wake of its aggression, to be replaced by gold challengers with their own dreams. Gilpin understood; he had experienced it all before.

Denverites proudly welcomed the governor. Their town might be mostly wooden buildings, none farther than an easy walk from unsettled prairie, and their society generally unrefined by eastern embellishments, but they held the future in their hands and sensed that they were part of something larger than themselves.

That evening the impressive two-story, false-fronted Tremont House glistened for a grand reception in honor of the new governor. The "thundering peal" of Denver's new cannon saluted each state and the "young embryo state of Colorado," and announced the celebration. "Excellent band music," mostly patriotic airs, serenaded the "very large congregation" that included a large number of "Denver's fairest ladies." Gilpin responded to his introduction with a "somewhat lengthy speech"; the *News* reporter noted his tendency in that direction. Even so, his listeners did not shift too restlessly because he told them what they had come to hear—a description of the miraculous progress of Denver and the great future of the region.

Even the present troubled condition of the Union could not dim either one. Only five weeks had passed since the firing on Fort Sumter in Charleston harbor had launched the Civil War. "The war back in the states," some Coloradans liked to call it. On this night it seemed a long way away. Three loud cheers for the Union followed the governor's remarks, then three more for Colorado. The band concluded with the Star-Spangled Banner. Colorado had welcomed Gilpin in its best tradition.

The June 1 issue of the *Colorado Republican and Rocky Mountain Herald* caught the spirit of the evening well: "There was manifest throughout, the best of feeling—all seemed well pleased with the new Governor, and his able address. They felt that he, being an old pioneer himself, would understand the wants and necessities of our new Territory . . . ."

Unfortunately, the enthusiasm of that evening was not sustained long enough to undergird a successful administration. The governor began well enough; without question, he had a variety of experience. Few could match him in that department, yet somewhere something went wrong. Future governors would have done well to pay heed to the troubled career of William Gilpin.

Gilpin's first order of business, and one in which he succeeded, was to establish territorial government. Gilpin's instructions before leaving Washington had been simply to protect the mountain region from secession; the extremely hardpressed president and his cabinet had little time for Colorado. The best way to achieve that end was to place territorial government on a sound footing.

The governor set off to tour the mountain districts and foothill towns, ostensibly to take a census, which was accomplished. The June trips did more than that, though. They displayed the enthusiastic governor and exhibited his government to the people. Boulder, Golden, Central City, Breckenridge, Pueblo, Colorado City and places in between—Gilpin visited them all, greeting people, seeing the new developments, and taking the measure of pro-southern strength.

One of the initial results of this tour and the census was to divide Colorado into three types of electoral precincts. The territory as a whole would elect a delegate to Congress (a nonvoting representative of Colorado's interests). Colorado was also divided into nine districts for councilmen and thirteen for representatives. An election was mandated. Politicians soon surfaced and campaigns were opened along party lines, with the Republicans taking on the Union party (largely Democrats, that name being in disrepute because of its ties to the newborn Confederacy). The Republicans won an easy victory.

The first session of the Colorado territorial legislature opened with the governor's address. A brisk September day with fresh snow on the Rockies to the west greeted Gilpin, and he rose to the occasion with his eloquent, visionary best. He first charged the legislators:

> The stern and delicate duty which is confided to you, is to create and condense into system and order the elements of stable government for this commonwealth of the primeval mountains, (to) become, in the march of our great country, one of the family of the American union.

Gilpin recommended this be done by dividing the territory into counties and establishing county governments to formulate a code of civil and criminal laws and to plan for an education system of "schools and colleges"; to create a territorial militia ("The citizen must be also a soldier, and armed"); and, finally, to encourage agriculture, mining, industry, and business. All these things must be accomplished as soon as possible. The governor issued no revolutionary call, recommending the path that every other territory had followed.

William Gilpin was not one to stop with mere mundane recommendations. He went on to trace developments of the past three years which confirmed

> The existence of the precious and base metals in absolutely inexhaustible abundance and variety; the universal fertility of the soil, as well upon the flanks of the Great Mountains, as upon the Plains and within the Parks; the uniform splendor and salubrity of the climate; the facility of transit and penetration by roads over all varieties of surface; these facts, conclusively established, demonstrate that our country is supremely favored by nature, with all the elements which promise unrivalled rapidity of progress, prosperity and power.

Only a few years would pass, he predicted, before the railroad would reach Colorado and bring with it an unlimited future.

Only one concern clouded this glorious future, and Gilpin, well aware of it, trusted that all Coloradans were equally enlightened:

> Our great country demands a period of stern virtue, of holy zeal, of regenerating patriotism of devoted citizens. It is to you representatives, and to the people of the young Territory of Colorado, that I speak. To exalt your intrepid enthusiasm is my aim, — With us are the Continental Eagles and the Continental Cause, immortalized by the purity of Washington, illuminated by the wisdom of Jefferson, vindicated and restored by the illustrious Jackson. Let us condense around those eagles and advance, devoted to maintain their purity and exalt their glory.

In a rousing climax, the governor exclaimed, "I pledge to you my cordial and intelligent cooperation in all that your wisdom and patriotism shall attempt."

The *News* lavished praise on what it called an able state paper: "In its beauty of style, smoothness and eloquence of composition, it can hardly be excelled by any writer of the age." Coloradans, the reporter went on to say, "may well congratulate themselves that their chief ruler is devoted heart and soul, to their welfare and prosperity."

18

The legislature responded with alacrity to the governor's words. Its session lasted two months, ending in November, and accomplished more for its duration than most of its legislative descendants would ever be able to do. Although it must be conceded that this body started from scratch, its record remains admirable, nevertheless.

One-hundred-thirty-seven bills were passed, including those defining county boundaries, locating county seats, organizing a militia, adopting civil and criminal codes, and incorporating a host of companies and the city of Denver. A state university was authorized and a territorial school system established, the rights of married women recognized, and a law passed for the protection of trout (Coloradans were already threatening their natural environment). The legislators also found time to send memorials to Congress concerning mail routes and the establishing of a branch mint in Colorado. The legal code adopted borrowed heavily from Illinois and put many fears to rest when it legalized the decisions of the extralegal miners' courts. The territory had been functioning for two years without a legal basis.

No conflict marred the relationship between the busy legislators and the equally busy Gilpin. As Territorial Superintendent of Indian Affairs, Gilpin worked hard to prevent any trouble, though his position was complicated by the unsettled national situation that had caused the recall of most federal troops from the region. Nor was money available to pay the Indian annuities in full, annuities promised by treaty. Gilpin pleaded for funds that were not available or were more desperately needed elsewhere. Fortunately, no conflicts erupted, aside from a few isolated raids. This period was one of marking time for Indian/white relationships; a time bomb was evolving for the future. Gilpin understood the basic problems, realized the temporary nature of present tranquility, and correctly warned Washington that serious trouble lay ahead. Two different cultures were claiming the same land, each uneasy with the other. The antagonists were products of a generations-old struggle, and both sides had hotheads willing to risk all-out war.

19

Establishing the territorial court system turned out to be a real aggravation. The Congress had solved all problems on paper by appointing a chief justice and two associates. Chief Justice Benjamin Hall arrived first; a strong union man, he and the governor got along famously. With the other two, the story was different. Unnerved by what he saw and heard, E. Newton Pettis left the territory within a month, while Charles Armour procrastinated back east until October, when he finally boarded the western stage. Irascible and unpredictable, Armour, too, saw few portents of a judicial future for him in Colorado and served out his brief term, rarely leaving Denver. Overworked Hall attempted the almost impossible task of filling the void.

In matters of less pressing importance, Gilpin and Territorial Secretary Lewis Weld sketched an official seal, and the results of a survey conducted the previous summer were proudly displayed in the first official territorial map. On October 8, bachelor Gilpin graciously presided over the governor's ball at the Broadwell House—"The grandest and most extensive affair of its kind ever known in this region," crowed the *News*. Lasting until nearly daylight, "altogether it was an event long to be remembered by the citizens of Denver."

Success appeared to be crowning the governor's efforts, yet in that very success lay the seeds of trouble. Gilpin was not indulging in flights of oratory when he warned of the peril facing Colorado from the Confederacy and of the need for a "holy zeal" on the part of patriotic citizens to repel the threat. He sincerely believed the danger to be great and growing, both from within and without the territory. He moved rapidly and audaciously to bolster his beloved Union's cause. With the federal government otherwise occupied, Colorado was left to save itself, with the governor's aid.

A letter to Secretary of War Simon Cameron, August 26, 1861, clearly showed Gilpin's concern:

> This people are inclosed in a circle of hostile elements converging upon them, and are utterly destitute of arms, ammunitions, or any weapons of self-

preservation. The Indians are hostile, and pushed upon us by enemies and their emissaries from the outside . . . .

The extreme desperation of our position, calmly appreciated will I know secure your prompt action. [Gilpin wanted muskets, rifles and field batteries.] Energy, loyalty, and bravery preeminently belong to the mountain people. To conquer their enemies appears to them more glorious than to perish.

There was, he warned, no place for Coloradans to retreat; they would be compelled to stand and fight.

The governor's anxiety about present and future rebels lurking in Colorado did nothing to calm his temperament. His worst mistake in judgment came when he assumed that all his opponents were either rebels or sympathizers. His unsubstantiated charges to that effect cost him public support. Fear, without facts, was the only justification for these accusations. Gilpin created enemies when discretion could have smoothed his way.

Gilpin's obsession with weapons had resulted in an "arms race" that summer, as he attempted to purchase as many as possible, lest they fall into the hands of southerners. Inflated prices, if nothing else, were the result. Cameron could not spare men, equipment or guns, leaving Gilpin with no choice but to raise a regiment of troops.

Recruiting men and officers proved to be the least of his worries; patriotic Coloradans eagerly rallied to the colors. Locating sources of revenue was another matter. Gilpin had no surplus funds but understood that he had the authority to "issue drafts on [his] own responsibility." With nowhere else to turn, he did just that, and thereby sowed the seeds of his downfall.

The initial drafts appeared in July, and before Gilpin finished, approximately $375,000 had been accepted at face value by merchants for supplies and other goods. This figure represented a substantial sum (most went to local businessmen) for an underfinanced young territory to carry. By mid-September an uneasiness pervaded Denver—would the secretary of the treasury honor the drafts? When it was announced in November that he would not, gloom descended. Drafts, already being discounted, promptly declined another ten percent in value, That drop was exceeded only by the fall of Gilpin's popularity. Months would go by before the Treasury Department finally acted and "thousands who suffered from the delay and uncertainty" could rejoice at the "rectification of Gilpin's stupid blunders" (*Rocky Mountain News*, May 3, 1862).

By then Gilpin's removal had been accomplished, thanks in part to the animosity of editor William N. Byers and his *Rocky Mountain News*. Seldom in Colorado history has a governor been so devastatingly caught in the middle of a vicious newspaper war. Those two Denver rivals, the *Colorado Republican* and the *News*, fought to dominate the community and the territory. Gilpin started off on the wrong foot when he invited the editor of the former, Thomas Gibson, to join him on his first tour of the mountains. The two became fast friends, much to the displeasure of Byers. Small annoyances accumulated thereafter, exacerbated by personality conflicts and the awarding of the territorial printing contract to the *Republican*. Byers eventually emerged as a staunch opponent of the governor.

No point seemed too small or insignificant on which to attack Governor Gilpin, who was stoutly defended by the *Republican*. When an article appeared in the *New York Times* (January 27, 1862) praising Gilpin and his efforts, Byers used it to criticize and ridicule him for the next two months.

There was a question as to whether Gilpin may have been the article's author, but whoever wrote it painted a grim picture of a territory "infected" with secessionists: "At first it was a life and death struggle—a mere hanging to life by the eyelids." The "excellent" governor bested the traitors and saved the day. The *News* overreacted as the following samples show:

> (March 6)
> . . . we cannot expect that he will display many gubernatorial graces or social attributes to his unintelligent and unskilled people, to whom he

returns [from Washington] . . . .

(March 22)

> One year more of Gov. Gilpin's administration would effectually prostrate every department of business in Colorado, retard emigration, and involve in one common ruin a territory. . . .

The *News* even went so far as to print a woman's letter rebutting the article's assertion that "males chiefly" inhabited Colorado. "We ladies have many friends in the East and we don't like to have it circulated abroad that we are not recognized, whatever, in our flourishing new Territory. . . ." Nothing proved too trifling or too petty to print; the total effect eroded Gilpin's image and respect.

Gilpin's friends and the *Republican* fought back. The *Republican*'s editor liked the *Times*'s article and charged that parties who condemned it were ". . . enemies to our vital interests—enemies to our constitutional government—rebels at heart. . . ." On February 27 Gibson robustly defended his friend's efforts of the previous year: "The courageous bold front of Gov. Gilpin awed the leaders of the Rebel gang." A newcomer to Colorado would not have known what to think of the governor, except that he was controversial.

Gilpin had left the territory in December 1861 to travel to Washington to secure payment of the drafts and defend his administration. He was too late and wielded too little influence now that the territory seethed with turmoil. Criticism mounted and cries arose for his removal. Late the following March, Lincoln's administration bowed to the pressure and Gilpin was gone, replaced by John Evans. The *News*, which had hailed his appointment less than a year before, lauded the removal of the "discredited" governor, who had shown want of judgment, overstepped his authority, and ignored the advice and confidence of the "oldest, most substantial and best known of our citizens." The loyal *Republican* defended Gilpin to the end, to no avail. Greeting Evans, editor Gibson was moved to say on May 16, 1862, "Although a firm and ardent supporter of our former Executive, we graciously bow to the rulings of the powers that be. . . ."

Gilpin showed a nobility of character and devotion to Colorado when he agreed to serve as a kind of governor pro tem until Evans arrived. Lincoln, however, had no choice but to appoint another to calm the territorial waters. His government faced enough problems without having to worry about a western territory whose mineral wealth it needed to help win the war.

It must have been with a covert sense of satisfaction that Gilpin spent those last months as governor. The much maligned 1st Colorado (the *News* relished recounting the sometimes destructive Denver furloughs of its soldiers) marched off to New Mexico and in March played a major role in repelling a Confederate invasion force. By May the Treasury Department recognized that the drafts had been a legitimate expenditure and that paying them was a proper obligation of the government.

Colorado territorial government was by then well launched and functioning. A solid framework of progress became the heritage of the year just past. Gilpin's success could not be questioned. Despite criticism, the governor promoted Colorado and was its most honored national spokesman. Colorado Territory and its people could well be proud of their somewhat turbulent first governor.

Gilpin eventually married and settled down in Colorado for the remainder of his life. In time the ex-governor came to be honored as a pioneer, and as the years went by, criticisms were muted and emotions stilled. Even harsh critic William Byers came to appreciate his old nemesis. At the turn of the century he called Gilpin an efficient and vigorous governor, but an idealist at heart. That stands as a fitting tribute.

The governor's family cannot escape the limelight of the office. John Evans' daughter Josephine later married Samuel Elbert, who served as territorial governor in 1873-74. Second Territorial Governor Evans' administration (1862-65) ended in the aftermath of the Sand Creek Massacre. *Courtesy Colorado Historical Society.*

Colorado:
1876-1900

Colorado fulfilled its mining promise during this period, emerging as the number one mining state in the nation. Recurring mining rushes created high excitement during these years. Leadville, Ouray, Ruby/Irwin, Silver Cliff, Aspen, and Cripple Creek were names that stirred men's souls and kept Colorado's name before the American public. By the turn of the century, gold and silver mining shared the limelight with copper, coal, zinc, lead and even oil. Colorado's mineral treasure chest overflowed, though some districts had already sharply declined from previous peaks of population and production.

Seldom has the state been convulsed by such an economic/political upheaval as the one that came with the silver issue at the very apex of mining's influence. It dated from the 1870s when the government stopped buying silver, and ran for twenty years as the price of the queen of metals declined, reflecting the outpouring of Colorado silver into a flooded market. Coloradans in general and politicians in particular knew the ramifications of the issue and what a rise in the price of the metal—"free silver"—could do.

Farming grew steadily and came to provide a more reliable, if more prosaic, economic base. Greeley's Ben Eaton showed the way the wind was beginning to blow when he won the governor's chair in 1884, breaking the stranglehold mining had held on state offices. Eastern Colorado had already experienced a limited agricultural boom-and-bust cycle, and farmers, undaunted, were coming back with renewed expectations.

Denver's population surpassed 130,000 by 1900. Thanks to Leadville's silver wealth and other windfalls, its residents had fine homes, buildings, hospitals, and schools, and the city had become the banking, business, transportation, and cultural heart of Colorado. Industrial Pueblo, with its Colorado Fuel and Iron and smelters, was second, and Colorado Springs, with tourism and its Cripple Creek connection, third. On the Western Slope and the eastern plains many other communities had high aspirations, but none could seriously challenge the leaders.

Change was the only constant during these years. Growth, economic ups and downs, increasing labor unrest, political turmoil, changing leadership, and the disappearance of the frontier affected Colorado. Still a state with weak internal finances, Colorado was an economic colony of outside investors, who controlled to some degree everything from farm land to mining property to railroads. And it could not stand alone when mineral prices and farm prices depended upon outside circumstances.

As the frontier days receded, Colorado and Coloradans were losing the things that made them different from eastern Americans. Denver looked like any other big city, Colorado's farmers marched to the same beat as Illinois's, and railroads evoked similar complaints from shippers. The pioneers of '59 were almost as extinct as the buffalo, having been replaced by the youth of the ragtime era. All in all, Colorado was farther removed from the Pike's Peak gold rush than mere years would indicate.

John Routt. *Courtesy Colorado Historical Society.*

The Last and the First: John Routt

Thunder rolled across the rain-blanketed Arkansas River Valley, crashing only a few feet, it seemed, above dampened Leadville, then echoing distantly in the mountains. To the west lightning silhouetted Colorado's highest peak, Mount Elbert, and its lower neighbors, while the afternoon sun peeked into town. This was silver-crowned Leadville, not yet two years old in this wondrous spring of 1879. Colorado had never seen its like before, not even in the days of the fifty-nine gold rush. Prospectors scrambled to tap unbelievable wealth; dreams sometimes became reality with the passing of a night. Ten thousand people had already thronged to the town's hastily built, crowded wooden buildings, most of which had never felt a painter's brush.

Only now as the cold, hard-driving mountain rain slackened did Leadvillites venture onto the wooden sidewalks to finish their errands. Even the hardiest individual found the 10,000-foot elevation taxing; no one needed the complications of a chilling drenching. Almost unnoticed among the multitude, a short, stocky man dressed in "mining duds stained with mine drippings and candle wax" went about his business.

The owner of the Morning Star mine had reason to rejoice—the month of April had fulfilled his greatest hopes. During those exhilarating days, his miners had finally struck an immense body of lead/silver ore after almost two years of searching, years filled with moments of doubt and despair that strained his pocketbook. He recalled:

> I went up to the new camp [1877] and was offered a claim called the Morning Star for ten thousand dollars, and closed the bargain before coming off the hill. The purchase money and the demands for sinking got me down to real bed rock, and for a time, with my personal credit nearly exhausted, things looked as steaked as a corn basket, but I had faith in the ground from the start and never gave up.
>
> You know a miner will never quit until he has put in a 'last shot' and I followed that rule. One day we broke into the 'blanket' of ore and my troubles were over.

Completing his business, the man returned to his mine on Carbonate Hill.

The owner of the Morning Star, like thousands of others, had come to the district full of expectations. Unlike most of them, though, he had succeeded. His name was John Routt, until the past January governor of Colorado. Routt, the only Colorado governor to work a mine actively while in office—picking, mucking, and hoisting beside his men—escaped to Leadville whenever his official duties permitted. Those duties were not so pressing in the 1870s, and Routt became a familiar figure in the camp as it blossomed into a genuine American phenomenon. Routt was, in fact, almost as well known and popular as Horace Tabor, Leadville's famous silver millionaire, who, coincidentally, had just been elected lieutenant governor.

The situation had been different back in 1875, when President Ulysses Grant appointed his friend from the Vicksburg campaign days as territorial governor. Routt was thereby given the honor of serving as the last territorial governor and presented with the opportunity to be elected the first state governor. Routt achieved the second honor on his own. He had hurried to the territory to defuse a heated political crisis, "harmonize" the warring factions of the Republican party, and put the machinery in motion for statehood.

Since the days of Gilpin, governors had come and gone, several accomplishing little more than to agitate Coloradans. It appeared that Washington was using the territory as a dumping ground for carpetbaggers or, what was worse, "broken down political hacks." Grant had felt the wrath of the populace earlier when he appointed another Civil War veteran, Edward McCook. Determined to use his powers to the fullest and play the customary game of spoils, McCook managed to alienate a good portion of Colorado's political community. Scandals erupted, protests winged their way to Washington, and petitions demanding his removal were circulated. Bowing to the unrest and pressures, Grant removed his friend in 1873, but McCook, unintimidated, raced to the Capitol to present his side of the story.

The president foolishly reversed his decision and in 1874 back came McCook, much to the astonishment of Coloradans, who thought they had seen the last of him. This example of carpetbagging proved to be the final straw. The highly unpopular governor became a genuine liability to the territory and the Republican party, which split into warring factions over the appointment of territorial officers and Grant's actions. As a result, the 1874 election went to the Democrats, an almost unprecedented setback for Republicans. Again, demands for McCook's removal mounted and Grant caved in once more. Thus was the stage set for John Routt's appearance on the scene.

Kentucky-born Routt had grown up in Illinois before enlisting in the Union army in 1862. Following the war, politics beckoned and eventually led him to Washington with an appointment as second assistant postmaster general. Tiring of this, Routt planned to resign and go west to Colorado when Grant called him to the White House. After describing the stormy territorial political situation, the president requested that he go as governor; Routt agreed. The forty-eight-year-old appointee and his family arrived in Denver in March, where Routt quickly turned to resolving some of the local and party emotional issues.

One of Routt's strengths lay in his ability to reconcile disputes. He also brought with him a reputation for honesty in his dealings with people. Both virtues were in great demand during his first months in Colorado. Several people

31

who knew him commended the new governor for three traits he would also require: executive ability, political sense, and the willingness to counsel. His predecessor had too frequently chosen to fight rather than discuss. Grant had selected the right man this time.

Circumstances conspired to favor Routt. With the federal government offering Colorado statehood (the enabling bill passed March 3, 1875), both local and national Republican leaders sought reconciliation and unification in the territory to ensure a Republican state. Coloradans in general were also weary of factional wars, discord, and confusion. Routt's unifying efforts succeeded. As he said:

> My first business was to harmonize these two elements [Republican Party factions]; they were pretty nearly equally divided. Of course, it never made any difference in anything I did, never took sides with either faction, but came out here and attended strictly to business, which was to do all I could to help the State and territory, to harmonize the politics of the territory and to do everything looking to the development of the territory in its mining resources and everything else. I treated each faction as nearly alike as I could.

Routt and the territorial leaders set in motion the process to obtain statehood. The first step was to elect delegates to a convention to draft a constitution, Routt and other officials being assigned the task of drawing district election boundaries, canvassing returns, and certifying successful candidates. The Republicans hoped to make it a nonpartisan election, apprehensive that the recent party divisions had not healed sufficiently. Democrats, who had attained their only political victories because of these divisions, refused this concession and carried the day. Much to their dismay, voters selected twenty-four Republicans and only fifteen Democrats as delegates.

Partisan politics, however, played only a minor role as the delegates set out to draft the document. Much of the work proved to be routine and majority agreement came rather easily, especially on those features lifted whole from constitutions of other states. Perhaps the most passion was generated over the issue of recognizing God in the constitution. Petitions related to that point created a tempest in a teapot, which was resolved by acknowledging a "profound reverence for the Supreme Ruler of the Universe."

Routt observed the deliberations, using little authority or prestige to chart the course of developments. By the time he gave his 1876 message to the legislature on January 5, an equitable constitution had nearly been written and the Republican party was well on the road to recovery. The governor adroitly called for all people to channel their energies into gaining admission to the Union, ". . . when, through the intelligence, energy and wealth of her people, she may be among the first of the States, as she has been the first of the Territories." Routt vigorously directed his energies in that direction in the following months.

In that last message as territorial governor, he called for equalization of the tax burden, pointing out, for example, that the valuation for sheep ranged from 75¢ to $2.50 per head, depending on the county in which they happened to be grazing. After recommending an appropriation to start the University of Colorado, Routt called attention to the fact that the state penitentiary, built for a maximum of forty inmates, now crowded seventy-five into its facilities. Concerned about the short public school year, which averaged only 107 days, he recommended the term be extended to no fewer than 200 days each year.

While the legislature went about its business, the convention finished its work and adjourned on March 14. Old-timer William Byers, who had been watching state-making attempts since 1859, predicted: "It requires no prophet to foretell what the verdict of the people will be." The next step was voter ratification of the state constitution, which came overwhelmingly, by more than 11,000 votes, on July 1. Routt then officially certified the results and notified the president, who on August 1 admitted Colorado into the Union as the Centennial State.

Meanwhile, Coloradans and their governor celebrated the nation's centennial and the "birthday of the Centennial state." The *Rocky Mountain News* unabashedly proclaimed Denver's July 4 "The Grandest Celebration Ever Seen in the Rocky Mountains." Routt and other dignitaries rode carriages in the grand parade, and he served as president of the day for the ceremonies in Denver Park. Opening the festivities, Routt congratulated ". . . you my fellow citizens upon what has been accomplished, and especially that we, the people of Colorado, can add one more star to the galaxy which now flashes forth from the azure field of the grand old flag." Special anthems, a centennial poem, and oratory followed as the memorable afternoon slipped away.

With the advent of statehood, the scramble for party nomination commenced, excluding United States senators, who would be elected by the legislature, not by popular vote. Among those names advanced for governor on the Republican side was John Routt, a somewhat reluctant candidate. He feared the carpetbagger label, a charge that tainted him as it had all recent Washington appointments. Neither did he emerge as the front runner or party favorite— that position belonged to Samuel Elbert, appointed and removed by Grant during the McCook imbroglio. Although other candidates received some mention as worthy possibilities, these two fought for the lead. With bulldog tenacity, Routt scrambled for the prize. R.G. Dill, a leading political observer of the era, claimed that Routt's ". . . persistent energy won the day, and mainly through his own efforts he succeeded in securing the nomination."

Routt based his campaign on his successes as the chief instrument in healing the breach between the Republican factions and as one of the principals in securing statehood. Not particularly a Routt fan, Dill curtly wrote, "Whatever of merit there may have been in these claims was not allowed to suffer by neglect, nor to lose weight in their application to Routt's candidacy." As Routt himself had foreseen, his greatest challenge was to convince delegates he had come to Colorado to stay. He met that challenge, and even Dill was moved to praise his "energetic persistence that was at that time a comparatively unknown quantity in Colorado politics." Once more Routt was hailed as a "pacifier of

Republican differences," the man who could bring the Republicans together and command their respect and confidence.

Colorado's first state political campaign lasted from late August until the October 3 election. Routt gave few speeches, but in one he made the mistake of saying that his opponent would be laboriously climbing over the fence while he would be crawling rapidly through the lower rails. Democrats lampooned him unmercifully for this silly slip of the tongue. Both parties claimed an early victory, as the results slowly reached Denver. Nearly a week elapsed before the returns had accumulated in numbers sufficient to make an intelligent estimate. Routt's apprehension was unnecessary; he carried the key counties of Arapahoe, Boulder, Clear Creek, and Gilpin for the margin of victory. The party also swept the state, thereby paving the way for two Republican senators.

Later governors might well envy Routt's first term. The legislature met only every other year, a significant reason that he had more time to go to Leadville to work his mine. Obviously, too, issues were not so pressing, although Routt and his contemporaries might have argued with that assessment. Less appealing was the two-year term for which the governor was elected at that time, forcing him to start thinking about running again or retiring almost before he had begun serving.

The Colorado over which Routt presided was slowly recovering from the severe national panic and depression of 1873. Gold, the cry of '59, still resounded through the mountains, now more a whisper than a siren call. Rumors of silver had begun to assay into fact as some new districts opened, but it had been over a decade since Colorado mining had caught America's fancy. Agriculture, too, had its problems; at the moment grasshoppers seemed determined to eat most of the crops. Nor had Denver reached the potential its founding fathers had envisioned. Lately, however, some signs of progress were evident. The territory that had lagged so discouragingly now picked up the pace of growth, giving credibility to its ardent boosters when

Denver emerged as a railroad center. Denver's success sowed seeds of envy virulent enough to force the framers of the constitution to call for a state election on designating the capital in order to avoid jeopardizing the statehood vote. For the moment, then, Denver was serving as only the temporary seat of government; so it remained until 1881, when voters overwhelmingly confirmed the honor.

Routt's two-year term passed quietly, much less stressful than his previous year as territorial governor. Reviewing his administration later, he pointed to what he considered the most noteworthy accomplishments. Taxes had been available to pay every cent of state expenses (actually the constitution had a prohibitive clause about going into debt). School land (sections 16 and 36 of each township), donated by the federal government to the states, had been leased rather than instantly sold to take advantage of the expected increase in value with further settlement. Compared to the scandals some states experienced from quick, sometimes fraudulent, sales, Routt's plan exhibited good sense and benefited Colorado. No stranger to lobbying (Routt called it "rascality") to secure higher appropriations for state institutions, the governor thought ". . . it would be a good scheme to provide for the support of our institutions of that kind early, so we levied a given percent on the taxable property of the state for the support of these institutions. . . ."

Contemporaries agreed with his assessment, giving him credit for grasping the changes taking place in Colorado in mining, railroads, ranching, and farming. A hard worker himself, he inspired members of his administration to emulate him. According to a story from the era, should the governor find any state official shirking his duty, the offending person would be told to "fish, cut bait, or go ashore." His virtues of honesty and executive ability made him much admired and enabled him to overcome the carpetbag label to emerge as a respected member of Colorado society. Frank Hall, who knew all the governors of this era, said of Routt that none was more devoted to the higher welfare of the commonwealth: "[His] management of state affairs was in most respects admirable and satisfactory."

Routt probably would have thought that a fitting tribute to his administration.

Analyzing Routt from the perspective of the mid-1880s, political reporter James MacCarthy judged that he had done more to hold the Colorado Republican party together than any other man, a fact that other party leaders often failed to perceive. His political forte, however, was comradeship, not leadership.

> He is not a person of large mental calibre nor high cultivation, but he has had an extensive political experience and within his mental scope he is a bright, sensible, useful man with a marked capacity for public affairs—affairs that call for the clever politician and the man of business rather than the statesman.

In MacCarthy's opinion, Routt displayed an energetic and capable mind, not a weighty and comprehensive one.

Conservative and business-oriented, as were most of the leaders of his generation, Routt could, nevertheless, fight for reform, as he did for women's suffrage. His wife Eliza, an extraordinarily capable lady and a natural leader, probably nudged him into supporting the issue during the state election of 1877. Not one to dodge his duty once his mind was made up, Routt appeared with Susan B. Anthony and Lucy Stone to try to persuade his fellow males to follow his example. The voters were left to decide this issue that the constitutional convention adroitly sidestepped, and they defeated suffrage.

In his 1879 message to the legislature as retiring governor, Routt pointed with pride to the state's vastly improved status over what it had been two years earlier. The contrast in mining, growth, agriculture, and investment was impressive, thanks in great measure to Leadville's sudden fortune. A glorious future loomed.

From among Routt's more traditional recommendations and comments emerge two that show the spark of a statesman, contradicting MacCarthy's assessment to some degree. Routt recommended the establishment of a state museum to save some of the objects being taken out of

Colorado. He called for measures to preserve the ancient ruins in southwestern Colorado from "total obliteration," strongly urging the legislators never to sell school land upon which such sites were located in order to retain them for the benefit of archaeology. Unfortunately, several decades passed before such action was finally taken.

Routt closed by thanking Coloradans for their support and the honor they had given him:

> ...it is proper that I should express to you, and through you to the people of Colorado, my hearty thanks for the honor they have conferred on selecting me to occupy the office which I am about to deliver to my worthy and honorable successor, and thanks, too, for their confidence and support while discharging its duties.

Routt's public career had not come to a close, however.

The Morning Star mine finally rewarded the faith Routt had placed in it; its silver made him a wealthy man. In 1880 he and his partners sold the mine for over a million dollars, of which the former governor received $600,000. His new wealth was reflected in a fine Denver home, a carriage, and a pair of horses that cost $3,000. The Routts entertained lavishly and fit nicely into Denver's social set.

Routt found the life of the wealthy mining man/investor unfulfilling, even though he continued to invest in mines and to experience the corresponding excitement and risks. Always a loyal supporter of Grant, including his third presidential bid in 1880, Routt played host to the Civil War hero on his tour of Colorado that year. The visit included a trip through the San Luis Valley and the newly opened Gunnison country. Returning to politics, Routt was elected mayor of Denver and cast his eye on a possible senatorship, which he failed to win. Finally, in 1890, with the party once more badly disarrayed, Republicans again turned to their favorite conciliator.

Nominated for governor, Routt campaigned as one of the state's senior statesmen. The Democrats attacked him bitterly; the *Queen Bee*, September 17, 1890, called him "by nature a ruffian, by education a cow-boy." In the end such political spite failed to obstruct a victory; the party unified for what would be the last time in a decade and placed Routt back in the governor's chair. Times had changed since the 1870s, however, and long-festering problems were about to erupt in Colorado. Especially threatening to the state's well-being was the continuing decline in the price of silver, the bellwether of the mining industry.

For the governor and the state, the old days were fast receding; a new generation and a new age were at hand. Routt insured Colorado two years of comparative calm before the whirlwind hit but provided no elixir for the ills to come. He must have found it satisfying to occupy again a position of power and prestige. He symbolized a relic of the past more than a portent of the future.

One delightful story marks his second administration. It relates to Creede, the last of the great silver excitements that thundered onto the Colorado scene in the early 1890s. According to a contemporary, the blunt and emphatic Routt exhibited as a "chief characteristic" an utter disregard for the third commandment (You shall not take the name of the Lord your God in vain.). Profanity was a language that Routt had reduced to a science.

The background of the story lies in a controversy over land title to the site of Creede. Angered about the uncertainty, some people threatened mayhem. Worried residents appealed to the governor to send the national guard before it was too late. Routt's reply, though not entirely elegant, was to the point: "To hell with the troops. I'll go myself." He did just that and arrived at the jerry-built camp in a driving snowstorm the same night that a heated protest meeting was just warming up in a nearby hall.

Without hesitating, Routt went straight to the meeting, mounted the platform, brushed the snow from his coat and glasses, and, rising to the fullness of his five-foot-two, announced, "Hell, boys. Damn fine day ain't it?" Disgruntled mutterings were the response, one of which sounded to a reporter suspiciously like "lynch him, you old scoundrel." Apparently hearing the same thing, John, never at a loss for words, replied (properly censored by the press):

> What! You will lynch the old man, will you? Well, you
> are a pretty lot of ... ..., ain't you? You are the biggest
> lot of damn fools in the United States. Guess you
> fellows could hang me all right, but you would be
> committing murder and would not get your lots after
> all. What do you really want, to kill me, or, after process
> of law, get your titles?

His courage, candor, and earthy language turned the tide
and led to a peaceful resolution of the dispute. That was
Routt at his best—fearless, outspoken, self-confident, and
willing and eager to face a problem head on.

John Routt did well for Colorado during his years as
governor. He helped establish state government during the
1870s, and, after a series of carpetbaggers, finally brought
respect to the office of governor. Through his actions and
administration from 1875-1879, Routt had improved
Colorado's governmental reputation, which helped to lure
investors and settlers. And, as he had promised, Routt
proved to be no carpetbagger. He spent the rest of his life in
his adopted state, serving as a link with its past and fading
frontier.

Once elected, a governor has plenty of work; Ben Eaton (1885-87) ponders some weighty state matter. This well-to-do Greeley farmer had come a long way since he nearly starved to death as a would-be San Juan miner in 1861. *Courtesy Denver Public Library Western History Department.*

Davis Waite. *Colorado Historical Society.*

Fiery and Feisty:
Davis Waite

The "gay nineties," they were called, but there was little to be happy about during the 1890s in Colorado. It was as near to hell as some people wanted to go. Trouble had been sneaking up for years, and when it hit with a national economic crash in the late spring of '93, Coloradans reeled under the depression that crashed over them and collapsed their world. Silver mines shut down, businesses failed, foreclosures and bankruptcies occurred daily, jobs vanished, the unemployed roamed in search of anything to earn some money. From the eastern plains to the western plateaus, the depression's pervasive and sudden nature compounded the misery. Twelve banks closed within a few days in Denver. Weld County homesteaders, defeated by drought and hard times, abandoned their dreams, and the *Silverton Standard*, July 22, made an attempt to cheer its readers: "Those who remain in town must take courage, there is a better time coming . . . ."

The price of silver had been declining for a long time, amid howls of protest from Colorado miners. Now it dropped from 83¢ to 62¢ per ounce in four days. Active silver mining plummeted; once prosperous camps were abandoned almost overnight. No state could have been hit any harder than this one. Colorado's silver lifeblood was draining away.

For a decade silver had been virtually the only political topic among Coloradans. Attempts to help it regain its former role, price, and financial status produced many hours of thought, debate, and discussion, along with scores of pamphlets and editorials. Neither of the two older parties, the Democrats and Republicans, was captivated by the issue. Unwilling to alienate eastern supporters and business leadership, or to stray from their conservative political paths by championing heretical, inflationary western silver views, they went their traditional ways. This left Coloradans and others of like persuasion in a political vacuum.

Such a circumstance never lasts very long, and a new group on the block, the Populists, or People's party, quickly latched onto the silver issue. Its members supported the "free and unlimited coinage of silver at the ratio of sixteen to one," based on the price of $20-an-ounce gold or $1.25 for silver. Coloradans took the party to their hearts and cheered it on.

Disenchantment with the stand of the two established parties, augmented by its own freshness and enthusiasm, catapulted the Populists into the center of Colorado's political stage. They advocated a variety of reforms; lest anyone misunderstand, however, in Colorado free silver was *the* issue. It was less a political campaign than a revivalistic crusade. Coloradans were experiencing a new phenomenon. Off they marched, singing their hosannas, awaiting the dawn of a new day.

As a result, the Populists did very well indeed in the 1892 election. They elected thirty-nine members of the legislature and the governor, as well as other state officials. The new administration had hardly gotten started when the 1893 economic tornado swept through Colorado.

In the governor's chair sat sixty-seven-year-old Aspen newspaper editor Davis Waite. This white-bearded, earnest firebrand looked every bit like an Old Testament prophet and behaved much like John Brown of Kansas and Harper's Ferry fame. At an age when many men had long since retired, this man, who had already coped with enough careers for several lifetimes, launched himself on yet another. An emotional person of intense convictions and lofty moral standards, Waite took the Populist program as his own and became its Colorado spokesman.

Populism promised far more than free silver; it was a movement by the farmer, the worker, and the debtor for such reforms as initiative and referendum, direct election of United States senators, a graduated income tax, and shorter hours for labor. These issues and more were revealed in Waite's inaugural address, which was enough to give nightmares to Colorado conservatives. The Populists in the legislature, however, lacked unity and strong leaders, which resulted in a harvest of problems for their governor, who had to veto forty bills.

Then came the crash that brought more problems and publicity to Waite. On July 11 he spoke in Denver to the Silver League convention. His short address closed with these ringing words, paraphrasing Revelation 14:20:

> The war has begun. It is the same war which must always be waged against oppression and tyranny to preserve the liberties of man . . . it is better, infinitely better, that blood should flow to the horses' bridles rather than our national liberties should be destroyed.

The conservative press plucked out what seemed to be a call for revolution and headlined it nationally. Ever after, "Bloody Bridles" Waite symbolized the ultimate revolutionary run amuck.

Waite had allowed his emotions and his rhetoric to run out of control; he never lived down the nickname that resulted from his intemperance. He tried to solve some of the depression problems but they proved to be beyond his political grasp or Colorado's ability to solve. Waite called a special legislative session to deal with the crisis, only to watch his program be ignored and the press poke fun at some of his ideas. It had not been a good first year for Governor Davis Waite. Colorado and its unorthodox leader had attracted undesirable publicity.

Undaunted, Waite dived headlong into Denver's dangerous political cauldron. Where others feared to tread, he jumped right in to advocate his pet reforms.

"There is blood on the face of the moon, and there may be blood to the horses' bridles and Cherry Creek may run red before the sun sets this evening," warned the *Weekly Republican*, March 15, 1894. Seldom in Colorado history has a more insignificant feud caused so much commotion, nor has a governor acted so erratically as this one did in what came to be known as Denver's "city hall war." Bloody Bridles appeared to be determined to live up to his nickname.

The sincere but stubborn reform governor directly confronted Denver's notorious political machine when he sought to achieve honest government and clean up gambling and saloons. The issue focused on the governor's appointive power to the three-member Denver Fire and Police Board, which controlled patronage appointments, removals, running the public safety departments, and licensing. Gambling and saloons flourished despite laws banning or controlling them. Many Denver property owners, businessmen, and lawyers benefited financially from those activities, and thousands more succumbed to their inducements. Waite sought an end to all this corruption and appointed his own members; how well he understood Denver's political system is unclear, but he had the gumption to take action. His first appointees were a disappointment; two were removed in June 1893, after a nasty name-calling battle. Now, in 1894, two new commissioners were, in the governor's opinion, protecting gamblers and prostitutes; they would have to go. The men refused to relinquish their seats without a fuss, and the quarrel was enlarged by the press and word of mouth. Those Denverites opposed to Waite (and the number grew each day) chuckled to themselves at what appeared to them to be an innocuous problem. Waite's own appointees argued that total suppression of vice was an impossibility, a conclusion with which Waite totally disagreed. Shouting gained nothing for anybody, so the matter was referred to the courts in early March and there it rested for a week.

The impatient governor startled Denverites by suddenly announcing that he planned to order the national guard to enforce his removal order. No bluffer, Waite went into action and ordered the troops to muster at their armory at

1:00 p.m. on Thursday, March 15. Denverites were incredulous and somewhat amused. Amusement became apprehension when it was learned that friends and supporters of the two commissioners planned to defend city hall against the impending attack.

On March 15 the defenders prepared themselves behind the massive walls of city hall, then located at Larimer and Fourteenth streets. Sharpshooters were stationed in the tower, and policemen, firemen, and special deputies—among them a generous share of Denver's gamblers and criminal element—garrisoned the rest of the building. Well armed with everything from dynamite to guns, they were not to be intimidated. Friends on the upper floors and roofs of nearby buildings also waited for the signal to open fire. A death trap would be sprung on anyone who came into their line of fire.

Denver and the defenders bided their time. At 2:00 p.m. the infantry and artillery troops advanced. It took them an hour to work their way through the crowd, which had grown steadily since morning to see the show. Young and inexperienced guardsmen unlimbered their two Gatling guns and two napoleon cannons, aimed them toward city hall, and waited for orders. Outclassed in experience, firepower, and manpower, the troops were easy targets, as were the Denverites crowded along the streets, restlessly awaiting the action. Inside city hall others waited, peace balancing on steady trigger fingers and calm nerves.

Waite hesitated—ordering an advance might mean a slaughter. But he could not stand pat; anything could spark the fight. Neither side seemed willing to concede or compromise. Behind the scenes, desperate Denver leaders besieged the governor, pleading with him to withdraw his troops. They begged him to appeal to the state supreme court to support his removal action, rather than issue a call to arms. Still Waite procrastinated, undecided on what course of action to take. A series of conferences finally persuaded the reluctant governor to withdraw, though not until a facesaving measure had been found. Waite called for federal troops to help enforce the law.

Five companies from Fort Logan had been conveniently alerted and were brought in. After seven hours the tired, cold national guard returned to its armory. Inside city hall the jubilant defenders relaxed. The exhausted governor, who said all day he expected to be arrested or assassinated, spent the rest of the night in his residence, guarded by armed men. Crowds gathered outside his home, proving noisy but not dangerous. The city hall war was over.

The supreme court eventually upheld the governor's right of removal but severely admonished him for his use of force. The two members having proven whatever point they intended and with no further recourse available, vacated their positions. Denver calmed down. The *Rocky Mountain News*, March 16, chastised both sides: the "wicked, indefensible, lawless defiance" by the city hall group; the "reckless, stubborn" chief executive—all were "grievously wrong." The incident boded no good for the city, the writer concluded, a "damnable spot upon its future and prosperity." Jerome Smiley, writing his history of Denver soon after the events, blamed the Waite administration for the miserable contentions, wretched wrangling, scandalous strife, and "one disgraceful brawl after another." The city hall war was, in Smiley's opinion, the "most disgraceful affair in the history of the government of our city or in that of the government of any other American city."

The governor had recklessly pushed the issue to the brink of disaster before he pulled back. The press criticized him unmercifully—nothing new about that—but his belligerent recklessness and near incompetence had played into his opponents' hands. Waite won in the sense that the new board did enforce the gambling and prostitution laws. A few letters endorsed his stand, and the local Women's Christian Temperance Union praised "such fearlessness for the right and suppression of vice." For weeks afterward, Denverites could talk of little else. They would long remember that March confrontation. At the very least, it helped slam the door on Waite's hopes for reelection.

The beleaguered Davis Waite hardly had collected his thoughts following the city hall crisis before labor violence threatened to erupt at Cripple Creek. Cripple Creek—that name was magic to depressed Colorado in 1893-1894. A life jacket thrown to a drowning man would not have been more welcome than the gold production of that district, which skyrocketed from one thousand to over two million dollars in two years. Its success meant jobs, business, and boom. Colorado mining was not dead; investors previously attracted by silver now succumbed to the lure of the state's gold. Colorado had a bright future, even in the midst of the depressed '90s.

Miners flocked to Cripple Creek from dying silver camps, while the mining era changed around them. Corporation control ended the prospector/miner's dream of achieving fame and fortune. Mining had become an hourly, work-a-day business, no longer holding out the promise of the days of '59, and with no new mining excitements beckoning.

The Cripple Creek mine owners were determined to make the best of the labor surplus dumped at their doorstep. As early as August 1893, James Hagerman attempted to increase the eight-hour day to nine hours for the same $3 wage. He backed down in the face of angered miners and their union, the Western Federation of Miners. The WFM, organized that year to represent the "hard rock stiffs" in an increasingly impersonal world, had successfully unionized the district, much to the owners' growing displeasure. Cripple Creek was ripe for trouble. There, for a time, the matter rested.

Resolved to keep the upper hand, Hagerman, David Moffat, and others announced that, as of February 2, 1894, the nine-hour day would be standard with no increase in wages. Unfortunately for them, Cripple Creek's two largest mine owners, Jimmie Burns and the legendary Winfield S. Stratton, plus some small mine owners, refused to go along with the edict.

High in the hills, at 10,600-foot Altman, the WFM's bastion in the district, John Calderwood called his men out. The strike continued for five weeks, an example of the classic rift between haves and have-nots. Misjudging the miners' resolution, the owners were forced into further action. That

49

came in the form of an injunction that restrained WFM interference and allowed "scabs" to come in and work the mines. Well-meaning but weak, Sheriff Frank Bowers of El Paso County tried to enforce the will of the court and ran into trouble when he traveled to the alleged "kingdom of Bull Hill." Six of his deputies were later seized by the strikers. He promptly called for state militia to maintain order. Rumors, fears, exaggerations reverberated from the mountainside to Colorado Springs and beyond. "RIOT AT ALTMAN," screamed a *Rocky Mountain News* headline on March 17. Denverites wondered what the state was coming to in '94.

Bowers' plea for help brought a heaven-sent opportunity for Waite to draw attention away from the city hall fiasco of only hours before. The governor told the sheriff that "calling the troops must be the last resort," but he sent them, and the first companies arrived at 6:00 a.m. on March 18. To their amazement, they found the situation not nearly so volatile as the press and Bowers had pictured it. Thomas Tarsney, Colorado's Adjutant General, was able to work out a peaceful agreement and the troops left three days later. "There was never any necessity for sending the militia down there in the first place," Waite said; "there is not going to be any trouble which the sheriff cannot handle."

The thunderstruck owners questioned whether the state government was on their side. They had never liked this cantankerous Populist and his ideas anyway; now they had proof that his pro-labor stance was something more than rhetoric. Waite had been an active member of the Knights of Labor in Aspen, and he was in dead earnest when he blamed the mine owners for the Cripple Creek difficulties.

March warmed into April, and when May brought spring to the mountains the strike still dragged on. The nonstruck mines continued to operate, while the stubborn "nine-hour" owners made no gains. Their patience was wearing thin, and the decision was made to take the offensive against the union. What better way than to hire some of Denver's ex-police and firemen, ones who had lost their jobs after the recent "war," as "El Paso County deputy sheriffs" to capture

Bull Hill. As the train carrying them approached Victor, the strikers dynamited the Strong mine's shaft house and boiler, raining wood and metal over the frightened group; the hired constabulary promptly fled. The furious owners, safely ensconced in Colorado Springs, ordered Sheriff Bowers to hire deputies to put down the "insurrectionists." He did, 1,200 of them. No need to rely on Waite and the militia now. Armed strikers awaited the deputies' arrival. Hatred knew no bounds as the two sides jockeyed for position.

The two opposing "armies" campaigned in the district, skirmishing and capturing prisoners. These belligerent actions were unacceptable to Waite, and on May 26 he issued a proclamation commanding all "good citizens" to lay down their arms and "cease all acts in violation of the peace of the state." The time for proclamation had passed. Waite hurriedly left Denver the next morning by special train for Cripple Creek. In the owners' opinion, his presence only made the situation more explosive; they wanted neither him nor his administration to be involved.

Waite met with the strikers and was appointed by the WFM local as its sole arbitrator, a Colorado first. Bad weather delayed his train's return to Colorado Springs. It was not until June 2 that he and Calderwood could meet with Hagerman and others on neutral ground at Colorado College. A four-hour conference produced an agreement on hours and wages but resulted in a deadlock on the question of responsibility for violence. Outside the meeting hall an angry crowd gathered; it seemed to have in mind lynching Waite and the WFM's Calderwood. The two men left by a rear door and safely reached the train.

The Cripple Creek district and Colorado Springs were in turmoil—union men throughout the state were threatening to rush to the aid of their brethren. Waite had to move swiftly and decisively to avoid a potential civil war. He first made every effort to keep union men at home, including one group that had already seized a train in Rico and reached Montrose. Waite telegraphed a request to go back, which they did. On the fourth he met again with Hagerman and Moffat. They reached an agreement which satisfied both sides and included a clause prohibiting discrimination against union or nonunion men in employment.

Meanwhile, the two little armies were tensely facing each other. The strikers, learning they had won an eight-hour day at $3, relaxed; a celebration was in order. The armed deputies, on the other hand, still sought glory and advanced toward Bull Hill and Altman. Bullets halted their advance, and Davis had to order out the guard because an army, recruited by the owners, now refused to respect the agreement. On the sixth the governor wired Bowers, "In present excitement I hope you will not advance the deputies. It may result in bloodshed, which can be avoided if time can be given for state troops to reach the field."

The next day the guard arrived, placing itself between the two forces. The deputies foolishly tried to advance. Waite stood firm, warning Bowers that the troops would prevent an attack, with force if necessary. The chagrined deputies backed down. When it became obvious the sheriff could not control his men, Waite, on the ninth, issued this order to his field commander: ". . . they are not a lawful body; are only armed marauders, and you must treat them as such."

At this critical juncture, Tarsney met with edgy mine owners and a settlement was agreed to: the deputies would withdraw to Colorado Springs, be paid, and discharged. The guard would remain to maintain peace in the district. That solution restored peace to Cripple Creek. The bitter 130-day strike was over and the mines reopened. The state had spent $67,174. The WFM exulted in its victory; the owners retired sullenly to their corner to await another opportunity with a more favorable state administration.

Davis Waite's handling of the Cripple Creek crisis contrasts sharply with his misfortunes in Denver. At Cripple Creek his clarity of purpose and firmness carried the day. Waite had shrewdly realized that nothing prevented a friend of labor from gaining a just settlement and keeping the peace. He played an unusual role for a Colorado governor: he was undoubtedly the only person who could have exercised the authority that gave the underdog union a fair break. One of his supporters called Waite "far greater than

Solomon. A man of this nineteenth century who has not bowed the knee to Baal (the gold owners)."

Few Colorado governors have taken the verbal or physical abuse that Davis Waite endured. The "Governor by Folly," as his opponents called him, saw little of his program adopted, and a bitter reelection defeat awaited him. Unsuccessful in either helping pull his state out of its economic morass or initiating a broad-based reform movement, Waite could be judged a failure. That would not be a fair statement; a battle had been lost, but not the war. The reform movement lived on. His courageous stand on behalf of Cripple Creek's miners would be remembered by both sides for a long time. And in 1893 women gained the right to vote in Colorado elections, thanks to the reform pressures of these years and, more important, the Populist legislators, aided by a few Republicans. They passed, and Waite signed, a bill authorizing an election on the question. Voters approved and Colorado granted this long overdue privilege, following the earlier lead of neighboring Wyoming. Contrary to the last, the petulant loser blamed the new voters in larger measure for his defeat. Thus did Davis Waite exit the gubernatorial stage.

Alva Adams. *Courtesy Colorado Historical Society.*

Democratic Warhorse:
Alva Adams

Eighteen-ninety-six was the year for the Democrats in Colorado; never before had the party enjoyed so much success. In the presidential returns, they have not achieved such success since then. Their candidate, the silver-tongued orator William Jennings Bryan, rolled up incredible margins of victory in the mining counties and elsewhere—Ouray, 2,108 to 20; La Plata, 2,764 to 85; Lake, 6,641 to 260; Jefferson, 3,176 to 300; and even farm-oriented Yuma, 351 to 158. Colorado unanimity did not presage national victory; William McKinley and the Republicans carried the majority of the country.

The silver issue guaranteed the state's Bryan landslide, as it had boosted Waite and the Populists in 1892. Colorado had become radical in defense of its conservatism a decade earlier, and the emotional flood had not run its course even yet. One beneficiary of this tide in '96 was the Democratic gubernatorial candidate, ex-governor Alva Adams, a conservative, but one who stood solidly for silver. The campaign reflected the confused times as voters claimed to be Populists, silver Republicans, Democrats, and gold Democrats; those political pariahs, the Republicans, bravely nominated candidates in the face of certain state defeat. The national party stand doomed them. During his campaign, Adams abided by the motto he advocated: "The first half hour of a speech is for the audience; after that the speaker is talking to please himself."

The campaign was a trying one for Adams, charged by opponents with favoring the gold standard and holding other views heretical to true silverites. They also attempted to erode his strong labor backing by accusing him of anti-labor sentiments, with no more success than they had with the silver question. The Democrats stood less than solid themselves; Arapahoe County's leaders were split and feuding in those days when Arapahoe included Denver. Adams won without their active support. It had not been as easy for him as the times and political tide might have forecast.

The result was personally satisfying, further enhancing the glowing description of Adams written in 1887 during his first term as governor (1887-1889): ". . . he is a bright, clever, young man, a promising man, a growing man." Adams's saga exemplified the ever-popular nineteenth-century Horatio Alger story, demonstrating that hard work brought success and wealth. Adams's success illustrated what Coloradans knew anyone could do with grit, pluck, and luck in that land of opportunity called Colorado.

Twenty-one-year-old Alva had come west from Wisconsin in 1871 with other members of his family on the recommendation of the family's doctor. The Adamses, prone to tuberculosis, sought Colorado's dry climate as the answer to their prayers, as it had been for others. Young Alva began his precipitate rise to wealth by hauling ties for the Denver & Rio Grande Railroad, then building along the foothills. Seizing the chance to better himself in the new town of Colorado Springs, he joined a hardware and lumber firm and within weeks had bought out his employer. When greater opportunity beckoned, he sold out and moved to Pueblo, opening a hardware store there. As the railroad extended itself, so did Adams, following it into the San Juans during the next decade by opening branch stores. By the late 1880s, this hardware merchant had joined the ranks of the independently wealthy.

This apparently dedicated businessman retained a robust interest in politics that dated back to his teens, when he accompanied his father to the Wisconsin legislative sessions. A winner in 1876 in his first Colorado political race for a House seat, Adams was tapped by the Democrats for governor in 1884. A man who had served only one term as a legislator seemed an unlikely candidate for the gubernatorial nomination. Strong, attractive candidates, however, were in great demand and short supply; the Democrats, a decided minority, quickly seized upon Adams, who easily met those qualifications and, as a bonus, was a businessman with ties in the East and on the Western slope. He lost the election but led the rest of the ticket and paved the way for a successful campaign two years later. R.G. Dill explained Adams's victory in this manner: ". . . personally popular, young, magnetic, eloquent and having an extensive business connection all over the southern part of the state," he broke down Republican fences in "every direction."

At thirty-six the youngest governor, Adams attracted voters from across Colorado. James MacCarthy, who could be caustic in his evaluations of Colorado politicians, praised Adams for his "altogether good" influence upon public life and his "considerable sagacity." As early as '88, it was rumored that the young governor had vice-presidential capabilities. An unidentified writer described Adams's popularity:

> The keynote of Alva Adams' character throughout has been purpose. He is not a great man, but he is a good man, a clever man, an ambitious and cultured man. He has made the most of the excellent talents with which nature endowed him and that is why he seems to be the most admirable man in the state.

In a day and decade when brash and sometimes vulgar stories of the *parvenu* titillated Colorado readers, Adams's family life embodied devoted relationships and unpretentious social aspirations. MacCarthy was moved to describe the Adamses in sentimental, yet touching, Victorian prose: "lives clean and useful, hearts pure and kind."

Adams's term passed uneventfully, the Republicans controlling the House and Senate and little of pressing importance being debated in the single legislative session. The governor signed several water laws, a bill prohibiting child labor under the age of fourteen, and one establishing a Bureau of Labor Statistics. The only matter that caused him some temporary grief was the so-called "Ute Uprising." A hit-and-run fight between a small Ute hunting party and settlers in the summer of '87 was tautly stretched by the press and panicked Western Slopers into a "war." Adams eventually sent in the national guard, which cost the state over $80,000 to subdue this melodramatic conflict. He overreacted to the clamor of press and public by sending the guard, but once ascertaining the actual situation, he strongly opposed the cry for a needless retaliatory slaughter and returned captured property to the Utes.

Except for this last expense, Adams had given Colorado a conservative, economically efficient administration, living up to the expectations of his supporters as an able executive. The citizen/politician left Denver in 1889 for Pueblo and his business, forsaking for the next few years any role in public life.

Now, at the start of his second term, he faced a much different economic and political climate. Colorado was only slowly recovering from the depression, and the soul-wrenching silver crusade had left its mark. Adams struck a theme of economy from the beginning of his administration by eliminating the costly inaugural ball. Then, having lived in the Albany Hotel during the first term, the Adams family rented Charles Dickinson's home for the second and was much less socially active. Adams made this promise soon after his election:

> My purpose will be to give a clean, honest, decent, business administration. The laws will be strictly and rigorously enforced. I shall strike so to conduct state affairs as to invite and encourage the investment of capital in the state to develop its possibilities. I shall do everything to encourage Eastern people to look with greatest favor on our state.... We are still unqualifiedly for silver and for Teller [Colorado Senator Henry Teller, a great silver spokesman], and shall keep up the agitation for independent bimetalism. Though we have not won this time, we hope for victory in the future.

This statement epitomized good Colorado politics from beginning to end, although one might wonder what easterners thought of the continued heresy regarding the defeated silver issue.

Another heritage of the recent past, labor violence, plagued this administration. This time the trouble exploded at Leadville, as the owners and the miners' union squared off in the second round of what would evolve into a twenty-year struggle. The Leadville strike landed squarely in Adams's lap in January 1897, through no fault of his.

Probably no community in Colorado suffered greater trauma from the decline and crash of silver than did once glamorous Leadville, the now tarnished silver queen. The booming, beckoning Leadville of Routt's day existed only in memory. Mines had closed and miners were thrown out of work, businesses failed, population declined, and feelings hardened between workers and owners. The Western Federation of Miners intensified those feelings when it made strong inroads, those gains being no more appreciated by the owners here than at Cripple Creek.

One result of the crash of '93 had been an agreement between miners and managers to reduce the wage scale to $2.50 per day, down from the standard $3.00, in order to try to keep the mines working. The pact stated that when the silver price rose to over 83 1/2¢ per ounce the old wages would be reinstated. By 1896 some mines had voluntarily increased the wages, others had not, generating a potentially explosive mood. Flush from its Cripple Creek victory, the Western Federation moved to organize the miners and was confronted by determined owners resolved to stop it. Demands for a uniform $3.00 wage got the union nowhere, and at midnight on June 19 the strike began. Mine owners responded by closing their mines three days later, thereby putting a grand total of 2,300 men out of work. Stubborn, unwilling to give an inch, both sides dug in for a long strike, which turned predictably bitter.

Violence and death eventually came to Leadville, and previous governor Albert McIntire responded in September 1896 by ordering in the national guard. The tide slowly turned in management's favor, abetted by the pro-business state government. Non-union miners were brought in and mines were reopened. The troops inhibited, if not destroyed, the ability of the strikers to intimidate or fight back. The guard settled in, the cost to Colorado taxpayers mounted, and the strike dragged on, while the WFM local lost strength week by week. These were the conditions Adams found in January 1897. "As soon as possible after induction into office I went to Leadville in the hope that some adjustment could be made between the mine-owners and miners." The governor took the night train to Leadville on January 14—the crush of official appointments and office seekers took second place in the face of this crisis.

Conferences filled the next day, from early morning until late that night. Expressing a desire to find the right and peaceful solution to the difficulties, the governor cautiously stated, "I am here simply to look over the field for myself and feel the pulse of the people and to learn from all sides the exact situation as it exists today." He met with labor leader Eugene Debs and Edward Boyce, president of the federation, mine managers, and local residents, trying to find grounds for compromise. Consultation was one thing, agreement quite another. The only thing Adams succeeded in accomplishing in several days was to have each side examine the other's propositions. Rejected before, they were rejected again.

Where did the blame for this impasse lie? Two Denver newspapers disagreed on the answer. The *Weekly Republican* pointed to the union, the *News* to the owners. Regardless of who was at fault, Adams's mission failed, and he returned to Denver intending to continue his peacemaking efforts. In an editorial on January 21, the *News* pleaded for an early settlement:

> The controversy has lasted so long and has caused so much loss and ill feeling that no public man can perform a higher duty than by endeavoring to end it in a way that will restore friendly relations between employer and employed.

60

Adams's best intentions went for naught, as did the legislature's, which appointed a special commission to investigate the strike. Facts came readily, solutions not so easily. Finally Adams ordered withdrawal of the troops, which were gone by early March, the same time the decimated WFM local voted to end its strike.

A beaten Western Federation retreated from Leadville, losing as convincingly there as it had earlier won in Cripple Creek. What the strikers wanted or offered was of little consequence to the owners and managers, who had already won by the time Adams attempted to mediate the dispute. Management vehemently refused to increase wages, rehire strikers on anything but company terms, or recognize the union as spokesman for the miners, the most critical issue. Adams was playing against a stacked deck. Lamely, he took pride only in the fact that "... I decided that the troops were no longer needed and ordered the militia mustered out of active service and sent home. The result justified my action, as the camp is prosperous and peaceable. . . ." It would be a long time before another governor made an impartial attempt; the unions found few friends in that office.

Adams's policy toward organized labor differed markedly from that of his contemporary governors. Opposed to using state troops to break strikes, he worked steadfastly for arbitration. In response to his urging, a state board of arbitration was established in 1897 and proved successful in ending several strikes before the end of his term. The mere willingness to meet with union leaders and treat them fairly broke tradition (most Coloradans tried to forget any precedent Waite set) and unnerved the business community. Fond of saying "a democracy has no right to fear a popular verdict," Adams was ahead of his time in his attitude toward unions.

Corresponding with the decade in which he governed, Alva Adams represented the transitional nature of those years. With roots entirely planted in the nineteenth century, he nevertheless came face to face with twentieth-century issues, no more clearly shown than in the "splendid little war" with Spain in 1898. He was the first Colorado governor to be called upon to mobilize and guide the state through a national war. Fortunately for all concerned, the struggle was short: "It wasn't much of a war, but it was the best war we had," said soon-to-be-president Theodore Roosevelt.

Never have Coloradans gone to war more light-heartedly and naively, infected by a Rocky Mountain version of the epidemic afflicting many Americans. War fever began boiling with the sinking of the battleship *Maine* in Havana harbor in February by a "terrific and mysterious explosion." Few felt ignorant of where the guilt lay; Assistant Secretary of the Navy Theodore Roosevelt thundered the common accusation, "The *Maine* was sunk by an act of dirty treachery on the part of the Spaniards . . ." Adams encountered difficulties in directing the excitement into constructive channels; by April, neither he nor President McKinley had contained it.

His office was swamped with a variety of offers of military assistance and advice, including calls for a special legislative session and mobilization of the national guard. Both before and after the declaration of war, the letters came and Adams dutifully replied:

> I am in receipt of your letter tendering the services of from one to five hundred Navajo Indians to fight . . . I am sure that the Government, as well as Colorado, appreciates this patriotic offer on the part of our red brothers. . . .
>
> [to Bob Mitchell, Cortez, April 7]

> The government will be very fortunate in the event of war in having so many men who are experienced in handling high explosives to take charge of that work.
>
> [to C. Hudson, Trinidad, April 14]

> I am in receipt of your patriotic letter of April 29th tendering your sevices as nurse. . . . If your services can be used you will be notified.
>
> [to Della Manning, Leadville, May 2]

I note your request for permission to organize a company of Spanish speaking troops. As our quota is now full I can not give authority for any more companies, although I appreciate very much the sentiment that prompts our Mexican friends to enlist.

[to Casimero Barela, Trinidad, May 12]

Because he had no authority to call for more troops, the governor declined numerous other offers in April and May, including a proposed regiment of Civil War veterans and a company from Crested Butte. The letters continued to pour in, nevertheless. None was more sincere than Denver's Thomas Nenehan's, which Adams kindly answered on May 11:

As you are not old enough to go to war, I would suggest that you stay at home and go to school. Perhaps, when you are older another opportunity will come to defend our flag, in which event I am sure that you will make a good soldier.

Although the United States was officially at peace with Spain, newspapers carried little on their front pages but stories that inflamed war passions. When Congress and the president declared that a state of war had existed since April 21, 1898, it seemed almost anticlimactic and long overdue. Coloradans by then were thirsting to get on with it, to march off and win military glory, and to defeat the "yellow rag."

Adams took no action until a telegram arrived from the War Department asking for volunteers, initially one regiment of infantry and one battery of light artillery, the latter soon to be changed to two troops of cavalry. The governor spent the evening of April 25 (the day McKinley signed the war declaration) until well past midnight with his staff, preparing orders and checking lists of equipment on hand against what was needed. The mobilization announcement met with no lack of public enthusiasm.

The first obstacle encountered in Colorado came from the regular army, of all places. It stubbornly refused to allow the guard to use the barracks at Fort Logan, permitting only camping on the grounds. This intransigence put Adams in something other than "the best humor possible," as he hastened to find a suitable substitute. Better that the guard should have its own camp than to accept such a miserly offer from the army. Arrangements were completed just in time for the arrival of the companies on April 29. The men finally ended up at Camp Adams in city park.

The still miffed governor inspected the camp and troops on April 30, amid a drizzling rain that did not permit a lengthy review. He made several recommendations to improve the men's comfort and returned to the capitol in his buggy. Unpatriotically, the weather continually failed to cooperate with the war effort; snow was followed by more rain and hail. Not until May 10 did "sunshine and balmy air" make soldiering seem like the fun the troops had anticipated. In their cold, damp tents in Camp Adams, the "pride of Colorado" were finding out something about military life.

Meanwhile, the seemingly simple selection of officers dragged the governor into the center of an emotional whirlwind. Adams announced that he was gathering data and intended to put the "best fitted" men in charge. Assisted by recommendations from the state military board and senior officers—and pressured by parents and friends—the governor drew up a list of captains and lieutenants. "I have done the best I could under the circumstances," Adams declared. Not so, protested two companies sorely aggrieved when their men were passed over. They thereupon refused to be mustered into service. Angered by such shallow patriotism, Adams hinted at "drastic measures." "Ample amends made by the hot headed young men" calmed him somewhat. Adams never was able to satisfy the Longmont company, even after he explained that the man in question was not physically capable of active duty, having only one leg. The company remained adamant and half of them went home, taking with them the regimental chaplain. Such were the trials of mobilization in '98.

Assuming the tempest had been quieted, Adams journeyed to Canon City, only to have it rumble again. The out-of-town governor missed the "number of citizens" who called at his Denver office on May 7 to protest his appointments. Returning to the city that evening, he expressed great surprise that such "a small amount of smoke should have created so great a fire," but he declared he would stand by his guns. He closed by saying, "However, if the Colorado boys are to fight the Spaniards, it is a good thing to know who are willing to fight and who prefer to stay at home."

Tensions relaxed after the impressive ceremony of mustering the national guard into the First Regiment of Colorado Volunteers. Drills, the bad weather, and the routine of military life generated news from Camp Adams, enlivened by rumors of the regiment's intended destination. When the weather finally broke and roads improved to "fairly passable," mothers, sisters, and sweethearts appeared in camp with cakes and pies for their "soldiering boys," adding a touch of home to the soldiers' lives.

Adams and the First Regiment commander were eventually notified that San Francisco would be the group's destination, in preparation for a voyage to the Philippine Islands. All hopes of gallantly liberating Cuba were dashed. Adams reviewed the troops one more time, bade them a formal goodbye, and left pleased and proud of his volunteers. On May 17 Camp Adams was abandoned and razed in two hours, appropriately in rain and hail. The troops marched off cheerfully to Union Depot to board the train that they anticipated would take them to fame and battle. A "stirring day," the *Rocky Mountain News* described it—the magnificent looking young men, "the flower of Colorado youth" marching off to war. Amid cheers, waving handkerchiefs, and the rousing battle cry "Remember the Maine," they rode off, leaving behind on the platform sad faces and wet eyes. The newspaper politely refrained from mentioning the rhyming remainder of the battle cry: ". . . to hell with Spain."

In three weeks Adams mobilized, equipped, and dispatched Colorado troops, an unmatched record. Because the legislature was not in session and thus unable to authorize a special appropriation—and because no federal money was being sent west at the moment—he had to borrow funds from private individuals to finance the muster, issuing over $26,000 worth of certificates. The governor shouldered the responsibility, overcame the nagging difficulties along the way, and, as a final gesture, personally paid for the identification tags worn by each soldier.

The Leadville strike and the Spanish-American War preparations show Alva Adams at his best—forceful, active, and concerned. Success did not always crown his efforts, as in the labor troubles, but he made a sincere effort to try to solve the problems. He could be very progressive, as he was when opposing public executions and capital punishment; at his suggestion the legislature abolished the latter, only to have it resumed later. It is not fair to label him simply a business-oriented, conservative leader. Neither was he a reformer of the type some Coloradans were already searching for. Adams exhibited characteristics of both sides and provided transitional leadership for a state and people unsure where they were headed. Adams's second term did not end his public career; ahead lay the most controversial election in Colorado's history—and probably the most corrupt as well.

Colorado:
1900-1930

Turmoil and depression, with a few high spots in between, might be the terms that best characterize these years. Labor disputes marked the course of the 1890s with alarming frequency, followed by the period from 1903 to 1914, when a vicious cycle of labor strikes erupted in the hard rock and coal camps. No longer a frontier with boundless opportunities, Colorado now offered little for the miner except dangerous, daily-wage work. The owners opposed unions, and the workers deplored management's actions. Chaos and tragedy resulted. All of Colorado and its citizens were the losers.

Gold, silver, lead, copper, and zinc production, which peaked at $50,000,000 in 1900, fell sharply in twenty years to a third of what it had been. As mining wound down, agriculture emerged as the economic mainstay. The old order gave way to the new as surely as the horse to the automobile.

Amid all the unrest of the century's first years came some proud moments. Denver hosted the 1908 Democratic convention, a promotional windfall that showed off its new maturity. And Coloradans on the whole remained optimistic, shown by their active involvement in the progressive reform era. They and all Americans looked around them and saw the need for reform in the promised land. Condemnation rained on everything from tainted beef to drinking to the corrupt city government system. Denver's "big city" political machine and other entrenched elements bitterly fought the housecleaning measures. Some rural Coloradans were equally averse to the federal government's setting aside so much of the state for national forests. The year 1912 marked the high tide of Colorado's reform movement.

Coloradans gradually became aware of the great effort to "save the world for democracy," which resulted in the boys marching "over there" in 1917. Women stayed at home to roll bandages and plant victory gardens. Before it ended, they had learned to hate the Hun, and that hate lingered on after the armistice in 1918.

Hate and bigotry persisted into the 1920s, evidenced by the "Red Scare," and helped make Colorado one of the Ku Klux Klan's national strongholds in 1924-1925. Hate alone did not produce these aberrations—change, fear, resentment, and a yearning for the "old American way" emotionally overcharged the social and political atmosphere.

Some form of change affected the life of every Coloradan. Automobiles, movies, and radios produced an impact unprecedented in more than a generation. Added to these were the social and moral changes of the 1920s. A decade of personal struggle underlay the exhilaration that Coloradans seemed to exhibit during the "roaring twenties." Farmers and rural people missed out on much of the jazz age; the new inventions, fads, and cross currents passed them by. The farmers and other rural Coloradans had been suffering long before the crash of 1929.

The era ended on the jarring, tragic note of the '29 crash and subsequent depression. It did not hit the whole state at once, but it touched everyone eventually. No previous depression had caused Coloradans so much suffering. The "Happy Days are Here Again" hopes of the 1930 hit song were years away for Colorado and the United States.

Campaigning and speeches are the life blood of any governor's career. William Sweet (1923-25) emphasizes a point for his listeners, perhaps during his losing campaign in 1924. *Courtesy Denver Public Library Western History Department.*

James Peabody.
*Courtesy Colorado
Historical Society.*

Jesse McDonald.
*Courtesy Denver
Public Library
Western History
Department.*

Three Governors
in One Day

ADAMS IS ELECTED

Returns are incomplete but his plurality is estimated at
nearly ten thousand.
We stand for Alva Adams.
Honesty and justice must prevail.

[*Durango Democrat*, Nov. 10, 1904]

PEABODY IS ELECTED BY FAIR VOTES

Face of Returns show lead for Adams—Elimination of
bogus vote in Denver will insure Peabody a safe
plurality.
Republican leaders do not concede the defeat of
Peabody.

[*Weekly Republican*, Nov. 10, 1904]

Although the reader might reasonably think otherwise,
these headlines refer to the same gubernatorial election, that
of 1904 featuring James Peabody and Alva Adams. Never
before or since has Colorado experienced an election like
this one, which touched off a bizarre series of events that
climaxed in the strangest political episode in the state's
history.

The year 1904 had been a wild one for Colorado, reaching
a high point of labor unrest and violence as the Western
Federation of Miners continued their decade-old struggle
against the mine owners. Each side arrogantly defied the

71

other and bitterly struggled for dominance. Sitting nervously in the governor's chair during 1903-1904, James Peabody had consistently used the full power of government on behalf of his ardent backers, the owners and businessmen, against striking miners. This fifty-four-year-old, highly successful Canon City merchant and banker, and the town's former mayor, acknowledged nothing of worth in the position of unions or the role of workers. Always a banker/businessman at heart, he believed every problem would yield to hard labor and loyalty to the employer.

The outcome of this philosophy was predictable: the national guard was ordered in to quash dissent, and neutrality went by the board when troops forcibly challenged the WFM. Rights of free speech, freedom of the press, freedom of assembly, trial by jury, and innocence until proven guilty were replaced by harassment of suspected union members and sympathizers, arrests, deportation, martial law, and guilt by association. Peabody and his guard battered the union wherever they found it. Cripple Creek and Telluride became infamous for violence and brutal retaliation on the part of the state government. In the end, the WFM was vanquished. The expense to the taxpayers for the two years of activity was $776,464. Less easy to measure but no less devastating were the other costs: trampling of civil rights and individual liberties, Colorado's acquisition of a contemptible reputation, inestimable personal grief and tragedy, and property destruction and death.

Though justified in stopping the violence and curbing the excesses, Peabody overreacted in a totally partisan manner and with one major goal in mind. The Vermont native convinced himself that he was only performing his duty: "I have done my duty. I have taken steps for the preservation of life and property, and enforcement of the law." If not the worst governor in Colorado history, James Peabody can lay claim to a position near the bottom of the list.

When the corporation-controlled Republican party renominated the governor, Peabody and his policies instantly became the central issue of the campaign. The

Democrats turned to their old war horse, Alva Adams, a longtime friend of labor. The battle lines were drawn.

A brutal, vindictive, heatedly partisan campaign unfolded. "Socialist," "Colorado mortgaged to Wall Street," "anarchist," "union tool," "money interests vs. the people"—these were some of the epithets flung at the candidates. "Peabody, Peace and Prosperity" keynoted the governor's campaign; "Peace and Order" was Adams's battle cry. Peabody was denounced for replacing civil authority with military law, for deporting miners and their supporters without trial or inquiry, and for usurpation of power and selling out to the corporations. Republicans accused Adams of encouraging disorder and alienating the working man while cozying up to the WFM, which, it was charged, represented nothing but socialism and anarchy. It was a spiteful, bigoted, class-baiting race.

When the votes were counted, Adams appeared to have won, with over 123,000 votes to Peabody's 113,000-plus. However, each party claimed fraud and ballot box stuffing on the part of the other. The Republicans had entered the fray weeks before the scheduled election, focusing on Denver, where the Democratic boss Robert Speer and his machine had things their own way and conducted elections pretty much as they pleased. In an inflammatory headline on October 27 the *Weekly Republican* raged about "TREMENDOUS FRAUDS IN TENDERLOIN." The reporter warned that "bogus names should be eliminated before the election to prevent a big legal fight." This and other accusations motivated Republican leaders to ask the Colorado Supreme Court for an injunction to force Denver officers and Denver Democratic party leaders to "observe and enforce" the election statutes. It was granted, and two court watchers were stationed at every polling place.

The Democrats, too, feared voting frauds, particularly in the southern coal mining counties where the large corporations, such as the Victor Fuel Company and Colorado Fuel and Iron, held sway. When the party petitioned the court on November 5 for "injunctive relief" to prevent election crimes, the decision was curiously delayed until the night before the election; even then, it was granted only to Huerfano County, which lay at a distance too far from Denver to allow the court's orders to arrive in time to take effect. Of the three supreme court judges, two were Republicans, who discarded neutrality in favor of partisanship—a fact of judicial life in 1904.

Reports of election irregularities proliferated in November and December. The supreme court, angered because its authority had been treated with contempt, moved to punish violators. It self-righteously limited its investigation to Denver, thereby ignoring Huerfano County and its officials. Simultaneously, Republican leaders filed a motion through the state attorney general for the court to direct the Denver Election Commission to exclude all returns from certain "fraudulent" precincts. The court instigated proceedings and ultimately threw out all votes, legal and illegal, over Democratic protests and charges of conspiracy. Six House Democrats and two Senate ones lost their seats in the process. Having jumped into the thick of the fight, the justices found more irregularities in Boulder and Las Animas counties, and two more Democratic senators lost their seats. Then they focused their attention on Denver again, rejecting the total vote in some other precincts. All the while, Adams's vote total was declining; the Democrats were in trouble.

Unfortunately, many of the charges contained a great deal of truth, and neither party stood guiltless enough to cast the first stone. The 1904 election, marked by fraud, violence, and intimidation, proved in no way to be a "free and full expression of the people." Neither did it represent anything unique in Colorado political life—only the more flagrant excesses gave this election unusual turmoil.

Allegations of irregularities went back for years and, as recently as 1902, Edward Costigan, lawyer and Republican, had described fraudulent voting and falsification of returns as "notorious and brazen." Even more emphatic was that pint-sized whirlwind of a reformer, Denver judge Ben Lindsey, who wrote a book about what he saw, revealingly called *The Beast*. He attacked corporation control and

Mayor Speer's machine. Among the sins Lindsey catalogued were registration of phony names copied from Omaha and Kansas City directories, crooked election judges, and "repeaters." In Lindsey's opinion, "certainly nothing of the sort was ever more barefaced."

In 1904 state politics sank into a quagmire of conspiracy. Legislative investigation eventually uncovered some of the slime. The Republican complaints were justified—Denver's returns were questionable, if not totally fraudulent. One of the party's attorneys reiterated Lindsey's and Costigan's accusations: "Election frauds have gone on unpunished by the courts in this community until their commission has become a quasi-legitimate occupation. It is a game of wits, the shrewdest manipulator entitled to the most credit for rolling up a fictitious victory." "Repeaters," paid to vote early and often, sometimes changed clothes between votes (women's attire ranged from bathrobes to evening dresses). The powerful machine, leaving nothing to chance, actually held a meeting to give instructions on how to be a "repeater."

Some of the repeaters needed all the help they could get. One forgot his "name" between the time he gave it to the election judge and the time he came out of the voting booth and was challenged. He accidentally mumbled his real name, corrected himself, saying he was mistaken, and walked quickly out. Another stayed cool under embarrassing pressure. After giving his name, he heard a woman waiting in line behind him exclaim, "My God! That's my husband's name." Without batting an eye, the repeater shot back, "Madam, do not attempt to convince our friends that you are my wife." After casting his vote, he strode confidently from the polling place.

The machine's diligence paid off; in precinct one, ward two, 118 Democratic and 16 Republican votes were found to be in the same handwriting. One of "Boss Billy" Green's precincts, with 100 legal voters, returned 717 Democratic ballots. Denver—Colorado's largest and only true city—was corrupt. The state's political and economic interests could not help but suffer from conditions in the capital.

In Alamosa and the San Luis Valley the Democrats busied themselves to an equal degree. Under the guidance of William "Billy" Adams, one of Alva's brothers, Spanish/Mexican Americans were marshaled and marched to the polls. Republicans protested to no avail. Another of Alva's brothers, Frank, was head of Denver's police board and part of the machine. Alva's personal ties were too close to proclaim innocence about what had happened.

Republicans had no reason to gloat over the unsavory revelations—their hands were every bit as contaminated. In the southern coal counties, mine owners had naturalized and registered thousands of immigrants, who voted as ordered. Joe Vetere, working at the Livesay stone quarry outside Pueblo, saw people come right out to the quarry with naturalization papers. One of the Italian workers told him, "We have to vote for Peabody or lose our jobs." Miners were intimidated, as the testimony of Tony Disneria revealed: "They would like awfully well to vote for Adams, but were afraid." Samuel White charged that he was fired for saying he did not expect to ask anybody for whom he should vote. Even in the hardrock districts owners applied pressure. A Cripple Creek miner was told that if the Democrats won, there would be "no work in this camp."

Not to be outdone, the Republicans established their own machines, albeit smaller than Speer's in Denver. The secretary of Huerfano County's Democratic Committee, James Martin, made these accusations against the G.O.P. "gang":

> It is a matter of general knowledge that people have been let off light in their taxes who voted for the gang; that they have been taxed to the limit and in excess when they voted against them. They have been boycotted in their business. In the protection of criminals, men have been protected for their political influence. . . .

Activities of this kind had obviously been going on for a long time.

Democrats and Republicans accused each other of bullying, challenging, and using delay tactics to discourage voters on election day. Both were guilty, whether in Lafayette, Denver, or other places where watchers reported such activities. One of them testified, "Well, the only grounds that I could see it was on was because there might be a heavy vote, and they was trying to take up time, or something like that. They were legal voters." As Mark Twain observed: "There has been a band of burglars operating around here rather actively of late, and I have no means of knowing with which party they are affiliated."

Colorado, of course, could claim no monopoly on those illegitimate activities, but they do raise the question of why they were thought to be necessary. Obviously, both parties felt a desperate need to win the election and were willing to go to any lengths to do it. Republicans could sense Peabody's popularity waning and worked more feverishly than usual. They feared, and rightly so, that if given free choice, Coloradans would defeat the governor. Corporations also jumped vigorously into the campaign to protect their interests. Most, like CF&I, American Smelting and Refining, and the Windsor Sugar Company, backed Peabody as staunchly as did the Mine Owners Association. In Denver the scramble for city franchises intensified the pressure for an election victory. As one officer of the Denver Union Water Company boasted, "We rule . . . the people have nothing to do with nominations and elections. We rule and we're going to continue to rule."

That hardly unbiased observer, Ben Lindsey, claimed that the people of Colorado were not free citizens—they were nothing more than "enfranchised serfs." His favorite villains—private corporations and public service corporations—were accused of the dirty deeds. In Lindsey's opinion they corrupted judges, juries, legislators, public officials, and political workers so that "they and their corporations may be safe above the law and in power to loot the people." After the emotionalism is winnowed out, grains of truth remain. The aftermath of the 1904 election provided plenty of fodder for Lindsey.

How was the election victory to be insured? The Republicans gave a clue to their strategy by appealing to the safely rock-ribbed conservative, business-dominated supreme court. The court itself had been modified in the 1904 election by a voter-approved amendment that increased its membership to seven. Two of the justices would come from the abolished court of appeals, and the governor would appoint two others. This raised the stakes a little higher, since control of the court had to be kept in safe hands.

Leaving no judicial or legislative stone unturned, the Republicans advanced on all fronts. Locked in a tie for control of the state senate, they took the initiative and challenged the election of two Democrat senators. The State Canvassing Board, chaired by none other than James Peabody, and totally Republican, upheld the challenges, to no one's surprise. The Republicans now controlled the senate. Their entrenched power paid decided dividends. Democratic lawyers were frustrated again.

When the legislature came into session in January 1905, turmoil reigned. The Democrats, united in their hatred of Peabody, held but little power as the minority party; the Republicans were fatally divergent. Some insurgents would not support Peabody, while others either tried to ignore the issue or stood stubbornly by their man. Peabody had already protested Adams's victory. The state faced anarchy if some compromise could not be reached, and inauguration day was less than a week away.

Amid the shouting and accusations, a compromise was achieved. The Democratic leaders agreed to let Peabody appoint the two new judges, while the Republicans in return allowed Adams to be seated without a fuss and dropped the challenge to Denver's vote. The shortsighted Democrats ended up holding an empty bag. Peabody came through for the party, provocatively appointing as one justice the lawyer who had represented the two defeated Republicans before the canvassing board. The supreme court remained safely in Republican hands. They had won another round.

Peace was temporarily restored and Adams was inaugurated January 10, praying that "my administration will make no history." Such luck would not be his. The Democrats, underfinanced, politically weak, and confronted by a Republican-dominated court, had taken a gamble on seating Adams in exchange for the appointments. They lost it, as the Republicans unilaterally modified their bargain behind the scenes.

The *Denver Republican* brazenly predicted on January 9, "Governor Peabody will be back in the executive chair before the Legislature has adjourned," which clearly showed which way it thought the wind was blowing. Even the *Durango Democrat*, with its jubilant headline of January 11, showed caution, "Adams is Governor . . . Peabody Back in the 'Briar Patch.'" The previous day's issue said Peabody would contest "and further embitter the people against himself." Apparently, Peabody had agreed to withdraw his original protest in exchange for financial support to underwrite a challenge of the election before the legislature. He cleverly waited until the Republican lieutenant governor was sworn in (the candidates ran separately in those days), since that officer selected the investigating committee members for a challenge of that kind. On January 18 Lieutenant Governor Jesse McDonald appointed a twenty-seven-member committee to hear testimony; eighteen Republicans from the House and Senate controlled it. Before they finished, they had listened to over 2,000 witnesses and collected 180,000 pages of testimony. They heard a lot of hearsay, secondhand stories, and startling eyewitness accounts. Enough evidence was presented to convince any rational person that fraud had occurred on both sides.

While that was going on, the Republicans enjoyed a little revenge for some of the Democrats' 1903 shenanigans. Those "dirty tricks" had included a challenge to the seats of two Republican senators by the Democrats, who needed votes to reelect Senator Henry Teller. In a blatantly partisan vote, Republican winners were thrown out and Democrats seated. Now, in 1905, the Republican-controlled senate voted to seat that party's two senators. High-handed maneuvers by both sides made a mockery of the Colorado electoral process.

The joint committee continued to wade slowly through the evidence and testimony. Democrats repeatedly challenged the supreme court's action in discarding all the votes, both legal and illegal. Handwriting experts had examined the Denver ballots in a somewhat cursory manner and on the basis of their testimony the court had acted. The Republicans, amply financed, had hired experts to support their accusations. Adams and his lawyers objected on various grounds and produced witnesses on their behalf. One of those witnesses replied tartly to being asked if he were surprised that his vote had been thrown out:

> I certainly was and I would like to get the experts here and give them a little tongue-lashing. I would just as soon have voted Republican as Democrat, if he is a good man, but Peabody should be ground under our feet.

The public in general would have approved that tongue lashing, as the hearings and uncertainty dragged on. Challenges and counter-challenges, conflicting testimony, rumors, and speculation—Colorado heard them all in those mid-winter days. Lawyers gloried in prosperity as the hearings continued day after day.

Sometimes an individual warranted headlines for a brief time, as did Huerfano County's election clerk Juan Montez. That particular county gave the Democrats the opportunity they wanted to prove Republican chicanery. Finally subpoenaed to testify, Montez refused to come to Denver until he first received traveling expenses. Adams agreed to pay those, and Montez answered the summons, without, however, a necessary ballot box from the Maitland precinct, a CF&I fiefdom. What boxes he did produce furnished evidence of unusual activity—poll books were missing and ballots were folded in all shapes—many obviously never counted. Ordered to go home and return with the Maitland box, Montez jumped off the train shortly after it left Denver. The terrified man won only a temporary reprieve, as he was arrested the following day and sent forthwith to Walsenburg for the box. When the box appeared, nothing was found inside; it had not even been used on election day, though the clerk had reported Maitland returns. The Democrats charged that CF&I officials had supplied the figures for the clerk to announce. Shouted the *Rocky Mountain News*,

February 16, "This is the most flagrantly corrupt incident that has ever happened in Colorado history." That may not have been the case, but it certainly described what had just happened in the recent election.

In response to earlier Republican charges and the supreme court decision, the Maitland precinct results should have been thrown out because of fraud. For that matter the entire Huerfano County vote, a Republican stronghold, should have been disallowed. Caught in a bind of their own making, the Republicans forsook the precedent that fraudulent votes nullified an entire precinct's results, did nothing, and the investigation went on.

Six weeks passed and angry Coloradans could see no end to the furor. Old wounds were reopened when some miners, summarily deported during the strikes, petitioned the legislature for compensation for damages suffered. That incident, along with press coverage of the investigation, kept the late Peabody administration in the public eye. Republican leaders grew steadily more worried about the consequences of their actions. Had they opened Pandora's box?

The harassed Adams, meanwhile, tried to conduct the business of the governor's office in as normal a fashion as possible. His official correspondence indicates an unusual number of requests for pardons. Apparently having pondered for some time why people turned to crime, he concluded that drink was a major cause and supported the prohibitionist position. He recommended to the state penitentiary warden that parole should be granted, if a man took a "solemn oath" not to drink a "drop of any kind of liquor. . . violation of this pledge to the extent of drinking a single glass of beer will violate the parole. . . ." Now that it was March, it was questionable whether Adams would be in office long enough to follow through with the idea.

The committee finally concluded its hearings but reached no agreement. Not one, but three reports resulted, one supporting Peabody (signed by fourteen members), one for Adams, and the third recommending that the office be declared vacant. Its authors confessed that "brazen, shameless and far-reaching frauds were committed in the election . . . and the complex and confused conditions of said frauds render it impossible for us to separate the legal ballots from the illegal. . . ." Three inconclusive reports satisfied no one, and the legislature erupted again.

The Democrats did not have enough votes to save Adams, only enough to defeat Peabody. The fractured Republicans had too few votes to seat the ex-governor, because the insurgents would not support him. A growing number of legislators wanted neither man. The stalemate could not continue—the uncertainty was ruinously affecting the state and its residents.

In response to desperation, the supreme court was petitioned to rule on the question of whether a vacancy could be declared. In an incredible display of judicial speed, the justices rendered a decision almost simultaneously with receipt of the request—it was "no." The legislature would have to choose between the two men. Peabody's diehard supporters had counted on that and hoped the tide had turned in their favor. Republicans, it was assumed, would not dare abandon their man for the hated Adams.

The assumption proved to be wrong. With neither candidate acceptable after all the sordid disclosures, a face-saving compromise had to be worked out. An ingenious scheme was contrived to circumvent the court's opinion. Peabody would sign an agreement to execute no business, make no appointments, and submit his resignation within twenty-four hours, after which McDonald would be sworn in. If that were agreed to, the Republican insurgents would support the ouster of Adams. Finally grasping the reality of his unpopularity and ultimate defeat, Peabody agreed to the plan. Rumor had it that some business leaders coerced him into taking the step. The choice was that or perhaps fatally splitting the party.

By March 15 the resignation was already being circulated in the legislature, moving one weary senator to observe morosely, ". . . if Peabody had kept faith with our members and had established a reputation for truthfulness, this would not have been necessary." The next day the vote was taken to seat Peabody, fifty-five for, forty-one against, including both Democrats and Republicans. Adams left the office, Peabody accepted it, and within a day miner, banker, and ex-mayor of Leadville, Jesse McDonald, became governor.

Four months after the ballots were cast the election of 1904 had been decided.

In southwest Colorado the disappointed *Durango Democrat* headlined its March 18 story, "THE JOB IS FINISHED. Peabody Resigns, Lieut. Gov. McDonald is Sworn in and There You Are." Three days later volatile editor Dave Day calmed down enough to say, "Unseating Alva Adams was a steal, an outrage, an assault upon human liberty and the ballot . . . ." The ever loyal *Weekly Republican* took the opposite tack on March 23: "Law and justice and decency in Colorado were vindicated and sustained. . . ." It ended by praising Peabody's "patriotic firmness" in suppressing WFM insurrections. Thoroughly tired of it all, the editor of the *Lake City Times* shamed both parties and optimistically prophesied, "Colorado's new day has dawned."

Peabody's and Adams's comments, as would be expected, attempted to justify themselves and sounded remarkably similar. "For the good of my party, for the best interest of the state I love so dear, the step I am about to take seems necessary from the standpoint of patriotism," the discredited Peabody proclaimed. Adams also took the high road: "I am for law and order, in the real sense of the phrase, and it is part of my duty to adhere to that principle. I simply submit to the outrage which could not be prevented."

The two contestants removed themselves from center stage, to the great relief of many Coloradans. Peabody, in the popular slang of the day, was "a dead one." Adams would run again in 1906 and lose. The beneficiary of the compromise, McDonald, served out the remainder of the ill-starred term, ran in his own right in 1908, and lost.

The most serious potential fallout from all the acrimony was disillusionment on the part of the Colorado electorate. As one said, "What is the use of voting? It isn't worth while to vote any more, I don't believe I shall ever vote again." Fortunately, that kind of attitude did not survive for long. With tarnished reputations, the two political parties crept out of the limelight. Undoubtedly, many of their leaders planned to return to their old ways, but that would not be possible—the 1904-1905 debacle sparked reform movements in both parties. It would take some time, though, to clear the air completely.

Speer's corrupt, powerful Denver Democratic machine, which had played such a prominent role in Adams's victory and downfall, was still around to bedevil Lindsey and his supporters. The corporations that had so influenced Peabody's actions did not surrender their power and would eventually have to answer to an angered electorate. The supreme court, which so loyally sustained Republican causes throughout the judicial proceedings, would eventually become independent, as it should have been all along. Colorado voters, who had been denied their legitimate right to elect a governor, did not rise up in righteous anger to smite the guilty ones. Without question Adams had been elected and removed in a purely political power play. Adams was no Moses who could lead concerned Coloradans on a crusade for reform; he had been associated with partisan politics and its trail of corruption for too long. That leader would soon emerge, however.

Lindsey described the 1904 election succinctly: "huge turmoil of injustice, subsidized treason and legal anarchy." Ex-governor Charles Thomas, who had served as one of Adams's lawyers, placed it in a calmer context:

> The compromise was creditable neither to the Assembly nor to Governor Peabody; and while the general public acquiesced, since it ended an unhappy controversy and brought political peace to the commonwealth, the general sentiment condemned it as an unjustifiable evasion of its duty by the General Assembly, which should have decided the contest upon its merits and awarded the office to one or the other of the contestants.

James Peabody often surrounded himself with his staff and state militia officers during his tumultuous two-year term. On this occasion, however, he is visiting the St. Louis World's Fair in 1904. *Courtesy Colorado Historical Society.*

John Shafroth. *Courtesy Colorado Historical Society.*

Fighting Reformer:
John Shafroth

Just as the foot-stomping melodies of ragtime replaced the sentimental ballads of the 1890s, and as prohibition threatened the domination of the saloon, so did America change after the turn of the century. Confident and always optimistic, Americans looked at the world with new zest and boldness. Awareness of a problem barely preceded a proposed solution, as impatient Americans organized themselves for "battle."

By 1908 the progressive reform movement was in full swing in the United States. It grew out of the turmoil of the 1890s and the revelations of muckraking journalists, who disclosed that America was not all that its people believed or hoped it to be. Fortified primarily by the urban middle class, progressives pushed for political, economic, and social reform in the cities, the states, and the nation. A mixture of Populism (without silver) and abhorrence of the abuses and evils of uncontrolled industrialization and metropolitan expansion, this movement transformed American life.

In the optimistic tradition of American reformers, progressives sallied forth to right the wrongs as they saw them. Confident of their ability to devise practical solutions to a wide range of problems, they looked upon government policy and action as the means to reach their goals—and promote general welfare and a larger measure of social justice for all.

Colorado headed the list of states in need of major reform; it had become nationally infamous for political chicanery and labor violence. The election of 1904 graphically illustrated the problem, but the troubles went back much farther than one year. Now the wave of change had reached as far as this Rocky Mountain bastion of entrenched patronage and corruption. As the national progressive movement swung into high gear, Colorado found itself planted directly in the line of march.

Nineteen-hundred-eight was another gubernatorial election year. In nominating a candidate, the Republicans proved they had learned no lessons from 1904; they selected the "winner" of the 1904-1905 farce, Jesse McDonald, and drafted a conservative platform. The Democrats challenged them directly by nominating their brightest reformer, John Shafroth, and ran him on a boldly progressive reform platform. It called for the direct election of United States senators and a direct primary election law, supported a state amendment for initiative and referendum, and advocated a state law regulating railroads and transportation lines. The progressive credo, giving power to the people and calling for more government regulation, was well presented.

Another bitter campaign unfolded. The Democrats found themselves constantly short of funds as a red, white, and blue "Democratic Special" locomotive pulled their campaign train on a whistle-stop tour. Shafroth refused to solicit contributions from corporations, and the party coffers suffered as a result. Even the candidate himself was assessed by the party central executive committee to keep the campaign afloat.

Not one to take platform pledges lightly, Shafroth guaranteed his listeners an administration dedicated to enactment of those promises. That kind of heresy alarmed Speer and the Denver machine, which had been beaten in the convention and faced growing criticism at home. Shafroth traveled widely to preach his message and won the victory, bringing with him a completely Democratic House and Senate. He said to a friend on November 6, "It was quite a victory, considering this is a Republican state." Not one to compromise his ideals in public or private, the governor-elect wrote the vice president of the Denver and Rio Grande a month later politely declining an annual pass for 1909:

"Inasmuch as the platform of our political party passed strong resolutions in favor of an anti-pass law, especially as to public officials, I deem that it would not be in good taste for me to accept. . . ."

What did Shafroth envision for his state in the years ahead? Understanding that times were changing and agriculture and manufacturing interests were growing in supremacy, he sought better development of Colorado's resources and improved transportation facilities to attract a larger population. William Gilpin would have applauded his efforts enthusiastically and endorsed wholeheartedly his statement that the state's potential "undeveloped is vastly greater [than] Colorado developed." Shafroth looked beyond simple industrial/agricultural economics to judge correctly that climate and scenery would be great sources of wealth: "The playground of the nation the state is sure to be." Together with educational opportunities, this attribute would lure talent and capital that otherwise might never come. Colorado had clearly elected a man of perception as its new governor, one who realized that much of the success of the future would be predicated on long overdue reform.

Rarely in Colorado history has an individual made such an impact in his lifetime and influenced future generations as much as John Shafroth. It is tragic that an individual of his caliber has been so largely forgotten and so little appreciated by the generations that followed him.

Like thousands of others who arrived in Denver in 1879, this twenty-five-year-old native of Fayette, Missouri, planned to seek his fortune in the growing community. A graduate of the University of Michigan, Shafroth came west to practice law, a wise decision in those years. Though a lawyer by profession, he seemed to have a greater inclination toward politics and public affairs. Starting as a Republican, an astute move in Colorado in the '80s, he joined the ranks of the silver Republicans (1896) and eventually moved into the Democratic party in 1902. As with Henry Teller, the silver issue motivated his metamorphosis, and they marched out together from the 1896 Republican national convention, leading a forlorn silver bolt. Shafroth proved to be a winner wherever he chose to run—he served two terms as Denver district attorney and from 1894 to 1904 as representative from Colorado's First Congressional District.

He was, an admirer rhapsodized, possessed of a fine voice, excellent oratorical powers, a strong personality, and an "impressive presence." That opinion was reinforced in the 1890s when Shafroth stood shoulder to shoulder with Teller as a free silver advocate. He even sounded like Teller in a speech at the Salt Lake City Tabernacle on May 16, 1895:

> They [Americans] are determined that no longer shall the legislation of the nation be against the common people; they are determined that legislation which cuts down one-half the money of the world as the money of ultimate payment . . . shall be righted.

> I have always been a Republican—I have never voted the Democratic ticket in my life, and yet I believe that it should be the policy of these Western states to herald to the east that we can no longer follow party domination if it is not in accordance with our convictions. . . . victory is bound to perch upon our banner in the year 1896.

Victory did not smile upon silver that year. Unlike the issue and many of its spokesmen, however, Shafroth did not fade away.

During his years in Congress, Shafroth championed a series of issues that placed him in the forefront of reform. One of the leading congressional advocates of women's suffrage, he could always be relied upon by Susan B. Anthony to introduce a suffrage bill aimed at securing a constitutional amendment. Not content with only legislative support, Shafroth repeatedly wrote and spoke on the issue, pulling no punches:

> I maintain that equal suffrage is right, expedient and practicable, and that the highest considerations of the public welfare demand its adoption. [1916]

> How can those who refuse to give women the right to vote reconcile their opinion with the form of government in which they believe? [1905]

The arrogance with which men assert that women have a sphere to which they should be confined must be galling to women of thought and action. Why have men the right to determine woman's sphere without even consulting her? [1910]

Here was a politician who unreservedly defended what he believed.

He endeared himself to both Westerners and Coloradans when he fought hard for House passage of the Newlands Reclamation Act, which has had such an impact on reclamation, irrigation, and economic development in the West. They also endorsed Shafroth's introduction of bills to open forestry reserves to mineral exploration, a move that did not increase the congressman's popularity with eastern environmentalists and President Theodore Roosevelt. Eastern reformers did, however, cheer his 1897 efforts to abolish the "lame duck" session of Congress. A generation ahead of his time on this question, he earned acclaim but achieved no action. His ability to perceive the local, state, and national impact of issues distinguished Shafroth from many other Coloradans in the tumultuous 1890s and early twentieth century.

Well aware of the new times, Shafroth stood in the vanguard of the fight for good roads, an ever more important topic as the automobile chugged onto the American scene. "It can not be a purely local question, but it is one where all receive a benefit, and that is solely from the commercial standpoint. When you consider that it is also important that these roads should be made good from the standpoint of pleasure. . . ."

This Coloradan attracted national attention and acquired a permanent nickname of "Honest John" in 1904. His 1902 election to the House of Representatives had been challenged on the same grounds as Adams's election as governor in 1904—Denver voting fraud. Both a House committee and Shafroth conducted inquiries. Although not personally involved, and despite assurances from Denver of no illegal voting, Shafroth found evidence of false registration. A man of principle, the disheartened congressman resigned on February 15, 1904 and returned to Colorado with an enhanced reputation as a "strong, liberal, balanced, but independent character."

This episode helps to explain his hatred of corrupt politics and why he pushed so diligently for reform while governor. Likewise he tried to tighten the procedures for campaign donations:

> One of the most pronounced evils under the present system of elections has been the undue influence created by corporations financing the campaigns of political parties. . . . Such contributions are often, in moral effect, indirect bribes.

"Honest John" endeavored to put power back into the hands of the people in order to curb such baleful influences, as did many other progressive reformers in the century's first decade. Then, and only then, could corruption, illegality, boss politics, and corporation influence be controlled.

Coloradans had at last found the man to lead them to the land of principled politics. This ardent, determined foe of graft and bossism spoke for and worked toward reform, a new crusade for Colorado.

Defeat characterized the crusade in the beginning. Shafroth succumbed to it when he ran for congressman-at-large in 1904, ending a political victory string that went back to the 1880s. In that scandal-laced election, his showing, even in losing, was one of the bright spots for the Democrats. Now his name was being mentioned for governor, and the stage was set for his 1908 campaign and triumphant reentry into Colorado politics. The road had been a long and hard one since 1879 and did not promise to become any easier as Shafroth turned his attention to a legislature controlled by his own party, though not necessarily in tune with his ideas or programs.

The 1909 legislative session tested Shafroth's leadership. For the first time in Colorado's history the Democratic party controlled every branch of state government, but that circumstance promised no bed of roses. In the senate, Republicans, joined by Speer Democrats, forged a formidable barrier to all reform plans. Here corporations could play their last hand; unless the governor played his cards carefully, Colorado could easily reinforce its image as "the worst governed state in the Union."

Not one to dodge difficult issues, Shafroth delineated his program, based on the 1908 platform, in his inaugural address of January 12, 1909. It brilliantly outlined his proposed progressive program and has had few equals in the years since for its number of advocated reforms. Ranging from direct primaries, through a campaign expenses law, to initiative and referendum, it was pure progressive Shafroth. In other states, governors like Charles Hughes (New York), Woodrow Wilson (New Jersey), and Robert La Follette (Wisconsin) embraced similar programs that gave the people more influence in government. These men were not radicals; they preferred to work through traditional constitutional channels.

To the proponents of vested political rights in Colorado, the reforms sounded like a call for revolution. They fully understood whose heads would roll. Shafroth made his position clear, openly accusing CF&I of campaign fraud and calling for an end to political contributions from corporations and individuals. Presaging reforms of recent years, he advanced what became known as the Shafroth plan, which asked that the state appropriate funds to each party in an amount equal to 25¢ for each vote cast for that party in the preceding general election. The idea failed to travel far legislatively in 1909 or later.

All elected Democrats theoretically pledged their support to the platform. Shafroth and his supporters had, in reality, to battle machine/corporation conservatives of both parties, with the outcome to be decided in the senate. Going into February, the feuding groups were still deadlocked; "harmony" meetings generated only name calling. Even the House debated endlessly. Public aggravation over the footdragging increased pressure on the governor to take action. He tried by meeting the Speaker of the House on February 13 to request no further delay on the direct primary bill. A week later "Mr. Democrat," three-time presidential nominee William Jennings Bryan, spoke to a joint session.

Supporting every single platform pledge, he challenged those who did not do the same to resign. The House finally passed the direct primary bill and sent it to the Senate, where it languished.

On March 9 Shafroth met with senate leaders and warned that "the people of Colorado are tired of delay in reaching the measures promised by the Democratic platform and the Democratic majority in the senate must act immediately." When nothing happened, he made another attempt four days later. This time the machine senators responded with a three-day filibuster. Conservative Republicans sat on the sidelines in silent but gleeful support. Still proceeding cautiously, the governor conferred with party leaders, only to see the bill crippled by amendments. That was the last straw—the angered governor went before a joint session:

> Seventy-six days of this session have been consumed by those who are evading or trying to defeat the bills containing these platform pledges. The conflict is whether party pledges are to be regarded as sacred or deceptive devices to gain power.

Angered by the parliamentary maneuvering, Shafroth threatened to play his ace by calling a special session.

At last, after more haggling, the senate passed an amended direct primary bill, only to have the House refuse to concur. A joint committee, commissioned to find a compromise, failed in its mission. Limited to ninety days, the session was nearing its end. Shafroth pressed desperately for action. Legislative leaders failed to rally the troops and both bodies dallied. Eschewing platform pledges, legislators indulged in horseplay—representatives attacked senators with wet sponges and adjourned to attend the Shriners' Circus. Meaningless rhetoric marked the session's final hours.

Thus ended the legislative session of 1909. It would be January 1911 before another one was scheduled. Corporations and the Denver machine had been saved by a coalition of Republicans and Speer Democrats. A furious, frustrated Shafroth saw his plans discarded with hardly any serious consideration. He had not kept faith with the voters, because of his failure to measure the strength and determination of the opposition coalition. The 1909 session could well be recorded as one of the worst.

Only a couple of campaign pledges had been redeemed, the most important one a factory inspection law. It paved the way for further reform, when revelations of inspectors led to a child labor law two years later. Meanwhile, Shafroth lashed out at his two obstinate, politically entrenched opponents, the Speer machine ("traitors to the people"), and corporations, which "are against every reform that has for its purpose putting government nearer the people."

While the fight raged and both sides licked their wounds, Shafroth carried out the usual gubernatorial functions. Like the governors before and since, he was inundated with requests for appearances, recommendations, speeches, charity donations, assistance in political matters, and freely given advice. A sampling of letters to Shafroth during the tense months of mid and late 1910 show that not all Coloradans were absorbed by the reform fight. Progressivism was all right in its place!

> If you want to make yourself solid on the Western Slope, recommend to the Legislature the building of a state road from Grand Junction to Ouray. . . .
>
> [May 9, from H.H. Singletary, Montrose]

> Being as we need rain in the eastern part of the State I will ask you to please set an hour for people to pray for rain. Everything is drying up here. PS. I am a homesteader.
>
> [June 20, Clinton W. Smith, Seibert]

> I beg to thank you for your prompt and favorable consideration of the application of Herr Max Huenten for a permit to kill one Mountain Sheep for scientific purposes.
>
> [July 8, C.S. Thomas, Denver]

> I ship you today via Globe Express one box of 5 nice young sage chickens. They were killed by me this A.M. hope you will enjoy them. I wish you all the success possible . . . .
>
> [Sept. 14, T.J. Thompson, Gunnison]

. . . the Methodist Ladies Aid of Buena Vista ask you to
please send some article, it need not be of more than 50¢
to $1 in value. Please attach your card.

[Oct. 15, item desired for a church fair]

And, finally, a lonely D.M. McKinney in Lyons wondered if
the governor could help him bring his family to Colorado
from Illinois. He had come here for his health (the climate
had "done wonders"), but, unable to find a steady job, he
could not finance the trip for his wife and children.

The resolute governor, meanwhile, bided his time. With
the progressive movement gaining momentum throughout
the country and scoring some notable triumphs, he realized
that time was on his side, even in Colorado. The previous
general election had given strong evidence that the majority
of Coloradans supported his position; they, too, were
growing more restless and vocal. Denverites gave a boost to
the progressive cause when, in May 1910, they handed the
Speer forces a stinging defeat in a water franchise election
and approved local initiative, referendum, and recall. Now
Shafroth had only to decide when to play his trump card.
Despite strong criticism from his own party and loud
condemnation from Republicans of what they charged
would be a costly boondoggle, Shafroth made his move and
called a special session of the legislature to open in August.
Backed by an aroused public (who could vote legislators in
or out in the upcoming 1910 election), Shafroth planned to
force the recalcitrant machine members into line. He
planned to have the House and Senate concentrate on reform
measures from the 1908 Democratic platform.

This kind of bold gamble took courage. Shafroth was
putting his own political future on the line, as well as that of
the progressive wing of the Democratic party. If the election
victory of 1908 had meant anything, it must now be
converted into action. The machine/corporation control of
the state had been shaken before but never toppled; the
governor staked his reputation on bringing the "beast"
down.

Shafroth had taken pains to cultivate support for his plan
throughout Colorado with personal letters to newspaper

editors who championed his stand: "I want to thank you very much indeed for these able editorials, for I am sure that they are producing great effect. The platform is sound, the measures will be effective if enacted, and we will get a return of government by the people. I hope that you will keep up the good fight." Few backed him more passionately than Durango's Dave Day, who became so carried away in his August 12 editorial that he called for "the Colorado legislature's extra session [to] wipe the g.o.p. from this state. The masses have already been food for the plunderbunds to the limit of human endurance."

When he addressed both houses on opening day, Shafroth did not have extremism in mind: "A shock to the moral sense, followed by a feeling of resentment, occurs when electors find that they have been duped and deceived." He simply asked that the Democrats live up to their 1908 promises. To his misfortune, the reform and machine/corporation wings of the Democratic party were still at odds. An old bugaboo, the party caucus, rose up to bedevil the reformers, especially in the senate, where the Democratic champion of corporations, Billy Adams, wielded his influence. That subverter of the democratic system, the party caucus, bound each senator to stand by the decision of the party's majority and vote as a unit. The old-line machine senators outnumbered the reformers. The scenario looked familiar.

Shafroth marshaled his forces and attacked the entrenched elements. The reform-minded newspapers rallied loyally behind him, pounding the theme of "the people vs. corporations." Supportive Coloradans wrote letters. The governor conferred with Adams and other party leaders, bringing to bear all the pressure at his command. On August 29 that darling of the reformers, former president Theodore Roosevelt, addressed a joint session and challenged his listeners to "be progressive." Nevertheless, the session dragged on, the House in Shafroth's camp and the Senate stubbornly holding out.

On the twenty-fourth day of the session, the Senate at last passed the House-approved initiative and referendum. This constitutional amendment could now be sent to the voters for their approval. Savoring his victory to the utmost, the governor asserted: "This is the greatest piece of legislation enacted by the general assembly of Colorado since the constitution of the state was adopted." A battle, but not the victory, had been won.

Pressing on with other issues, the governor butted heads with the caucus, where binding decisions were made out of the public eye. "The caucus must be smashed," proclaimed the *Denver Post* on September 30, a pronouncement echoed by the *Rocky Mountain News* a few days later: "In the open forum every man of honor can express his integrity. In the open forum every man of dishonor will be compelled to expose his treachery." Those words came far too late; by then, the caucus had prevailed. Shafroth did win a direct primary law, only to see much of the rest of the platform pledges gutted by corporation/machine amendments; he vetoed the bastard bills. As the session dragged on inconclusively, demands increased for its adjournment. With the fall political campaign in full swing, legislative momentum being lost, and expenses mounting ($82,000 total), this appeared to be the best solution.

Shafroth and the progressives had achieved less than they predicted and less than Colorado needed. Still, a breakthrough had been achieved, and the campaign of 1910 promised to make reform the issue. Victory might soon be attainable.

The Democrats' state convention replayed the special session, as Shafroth's opponents tried to discredit the governor and his efforts. Although far from being assured renomination, Shafroth eventually came out the winner in a "rotten" convention that featured a dog fight against the fading Speer machine and its corporation allies. Appalled by the reform legislation, they feared its effects on the future of their alliance.

The candidate took his case to a receptive public. A Denver real estate man and erstwhile Republican wrote Shafroth on September 17: "You will have the support of myself and family and such Republicans as I can influence, irrespective of any future nominee for the office. This sentiment is being expressed by many Republicans." The Republicans, as badly divided as the Democrats between the old guard and the young turks, finally adopted a moderate platform and candidate. It did them little good.

Coloradans were in a mood to follow their governor and support his program. His special campaign train took him throughout the state to defend his actions and blast his critics. Urging people to vote, Shafroth hammered on his primary theme—he was fighting for the people and their right to govern themselves. Republican countercharges, which claimed that initiative and referendum undermined representative government and could produce class government (in this case, the wrong class!) sounded weak. With elements of both the nineteenth and twentieth centuries, the campaign progressed with "monster torch light" parades, rallies, and speeches; cheers greeted Shafroth, who defended himself and attacked extravagances of past Republican administrations.

It all worked to his advantage. Initiative and referendum were passed overwhelmingly and Shafroth won with fifty-four percent of the vote. He would serve out the second term and then be elected United States senator. His accomplishments were many, but none was more significant than enactment of the first progressive legislation in Colorado's history, over the protests and delaying tactics of corporation/machine interests of both parties. The second administration produced the reforms Shafroth had hoped to achieve earlier—the harvest of those bitter struggles and disappointments.

This high-minded, adroit politician had played the political game well and could be credited with a score of achievements. During the surge of state and national reform in 1911-1912, no state ranked above Colorado. As a result of "Honest John's" efforts and initiated action, Colorado achieved a campaign expenses law, a tax commission, regulation of child and woman labor, the Australian or headless ballot, a state conservation commission, coal mine inspection law, home rule for cities and towns, recall of officials, a reorganized civil service commission, and recall of judicial decisions. This was popular government at its best.

Shafroth pointed proudly to the fact that there had been no increase in property taxes and that government expenses had been held down. No penny pincher, though, Shafroth made sure that education received generous support during his administration, as did all state institutions. The removal of the ninety-day limit on legislative sessions promised to aid future governors in securing their programs.

Although the battle had not been completely won, a good start had been made in reducing corporation control over Colorado. The people were, however, unprepared for the political power that had been handed to them by the reformers. They would have to be educated to accept the responsibilities. These, however, were small defects that were decidedly outweighed by the advantages.

John Shafroth deserved the thanks of all Coloradans for the crusade he waged on their behalf. He ranks with his more illustrious contemporaries, such as Roosevelt, La Follette, and Wilson, in his advocacy of progressivism, effective leadership, and success in achieving his goals. No Colorado governor before him had been so successful in rallying the people to the cause of reform.

Photographic Essay: Colorado Governors

Governor! People expect the person who wins that title to fill many roles: administrator, politician, leader, orator, state representative and defender of the "faith," public servant available for any and all local festivities, instant recaller of names and faces, and a paragon to venerate. The office carries awesome time pressures that take one away from home and family. Steve McNichols said, "People expect an awful lot more from you than they ought to in terms of where you go."

The job contains its moments of joy and sorrow, exhilaration and ennui, and wins and losses. No person can lay claim to it as a lifetime occupation. Most likely, none of those who have held it would welcome living in the state's "fish bowl" for that many years.

Coloradans of the nineteenth century typically saw their governor only on ceremonial occasions or in stylized portraits. As the years have gone by, more candid photographs have been taken and preserved, showing the many facets of the office and the individuals who held it. The purpose of this photographic essay is to reveal a view that is different from the formal, structured life so often portrayed. Like the rest of the book, the intention is to present a sampling, so that the reader may come away with a better comprehension of the whole and, in this particular case, a fleeting image of Colorado's yesterdays and some of its governors.

Radio, and later television, dramatically revised the method by which the governor presented himself to Coloradans. "Big Ed" Johnson speaks over KOA in Denver in the mid-1930s. *Courtesy Denver Public Library Western History Department.*

Ralph Carr receives help from two young friends in signing this 1942 proclamation, a ceremonial part of every governor's life. *Courtesy Denver Public Library Western History Department.*

More and more in the twentieth century, Colorado governors have been playing a national as well as a state leadership role. Here John Love heads a Rockefeller-for-President rally in July 1968. *Courtesy* Denver Post.

Governors have been asked to perform unusual chores. John Shafroth ceremoniously kicks the ball to start this football game, perhaps a contest between those onetime arch rivals, the University of Colorado and the Colorado School of Mines. *Courtesy Amon Carter Museum.*

The two gentlemen in top hats, James Orman (1901-03) and President Theodore Roosevelt, represent state and federal leadership. Roosevelt visited Colorado on several occasions. *Courtesy Colorado Historical Society.*

Visiting dignitaries and delegations routinely appear to meet the governor. Clarence Morley looks a little tentative as he is about to receive a gift of flowers from this young Blackfoot woman. *Courtesy Colorado Historical Society.*

Steve McNichols and five former governors turn a spadeful of dirt to cover the centennial time capsule during the 1959 "Rush to the Rockies" celebration. From left to right: Teller Ammons (1937-39), Dan Thornton (1951-55), Lee Knous (1947-50), Walter Johnson (1950-51), McNichols, and John Vivian (1943-47). *Courtesy* Denver Post.

Coloradans expect their governor to visit them on special occasions or during county fair time. Dan Thornton's trademark was his pipe, and Gunnison was this transplanted Texan's home county. *Courtesy Amon Carter Museum.*

A western legend, Buffalo Bill Cody, greets George Carlson (1915-17), while Elias Ammons (1913-15) and their wives look on at the Denver Auditorium. *Courtesy Amon Carter Museum.*

Governors receive a variety of gifts. Billy Adams (1927-33) is modeling boxing gloves given to him by heavyweight champion Gene Tunney. Adams's secretary, Ben Poxson, stands at left. *Courtesy Ben Poxson.*

When a Colorado governor and his family go out they tend to draw a crowd. Jesse McDonald and his wife are visiting Boulder's Chautauqua this day. *Courtesy Denver Public Library Western History Department.*

A jogging governor would have been inconceivable in the nineteenth century or, for that matter, in the first half of the twentieth. Times change, and now it is not unusual to read about Richard Lamm running rivers on a raft or participating in a long-distance race. Here, he is shown running a course near Durango. *Courtesy* Durango Herald.

A long day of public appearances tires even the most enthusiastic campaigner. John Vanderhoof (1973-75) looks exhausted after a day in Durango. *Courtesy* Durango Herald.

109

Clarence Morley. *Courtesy Colorado Historical Society.*

The Klan's Choice: Clarence J. Morley

Clarence Morley's name fails to merit a nod of recognition today, and it is probably just as well. He ranks as the weakest and least appealing of all of Colorado's governors. His was not an undeserved reputation; nothing in his career before or after his two-year term saves him from that ignominious label. How did Colorado elect such a man?

His gubernatorial failure was not Morley's alone. Coloradans must carry a large share of the blame, and the 1920s themselves proved conducive to the rise of this type of nonentity. Bigotry, social upheaval, and hatred produced the atmosphere that gave Morley to the state. The only consolation, which might serve to ease the disgrace somewhat, is that he was not so bad as he could have been.

The general unrest of Morley's era and the emergence of intense emotional biases extended back several decades to the silver crusade and the Populist party. The progressive years, with all their reforms and agitation, did nothing to calm the troubled waters. World War I added more turbulence. Coloradans might have stopped vilifying the Hun on Armistice Day, 1918, but they did not stop hating. A disturbing sign of the times surfaced with the anti-communist "red scare," which swept the state in the immediate postwar years. Its most dramatic manifestation came during the summer of 1920, when unionized employees of the Denver Tramway Company struck to protest wage cuts. Violence exploded, sending rioting mobs storming through downtown Denver. Within a month of this deplorable incident, public hysteria seemed to have run its course.

In that kind of setting, the so-called "roaring twenties" took wing. This decade of change, law breaking, innovation, and economic tribulation for rural and blue-collar Colorado set many Coloradans on tension's edge. Speakeasies, liberated women, relaxed moral standards, bootlegging, provocative movies, the Scopes trial, the Warren G. Harding scandals, the Charleston, the Tin Lizzie, jazz, decline in church attendance—what was happening to the state and the nation? It appeared that they had abandoned the morality and the patriotism which had once bedrocked the country.

For years a concerned minority had believed just that and feared the consequences of such profligate living. They sought something that would uphold their traditional concepts and keep America on track. They needed only leaders to help them express their frustrations in a manner that would have some impact.

That leadership readily appeared in the form of the Ku Klux Klan organization, which was making an insidious comeback in the nineteen teens and twenties. It had suffered a deserved collapse during the reconstruction years after the Civil War. Now it appealed to "reform" elements of the South, the Midwest, and some areas of the West; Colorado emerged as one of its major strongholds. Taking its cue from the tenor of the times, the Klan sallied forth as the most disruptive force on the state political scene. Anti-foreign, anti-Catholic, anti-Jewish, anti-black, pro-Anglo-Saxon white Protestant American, savior of "old time religion," and upholder of law and order and morality, the KKK took fire. From Durango to Julesburg it organized, marched, rallied, proclaimed its program, and burned its crosses. Fremont County, the Denver area, and the Fort Collins and Greeley region provided strong nuclei around which to grow.

. The capital city, in particular, fell victim to the slick Klan appeal; there its diversified membership cut across occupational lines. Business and professional men lent the Klan a measure of respectability, as did the women's auxiliary, which contributed its share of charitable acts (only to acceptable people, of course). Monday night cross burning rallies atop Golden's Lookout Mountain provided excitement and demonstrated the group's power. The Klan had come to change the course of Colorado and push the state onto a warped, bigoted track to the future.

Grand Dragon of the state organization, the dynamic, resourceful Dr. John Galen Locke, emerged as a force to be reckoned with in Colorado. He masterminded the KKK's rise to power and impressed those who came in contact with him. As a young man, Ben Poxson vividly remembered his meeting with the Grand Dragon:

> I think he was just obsessed with power. He was quite a domineering fellow. I know Dr. Rex and I sat in his office, which was in a building now gone, right adjacent to the Denver Athletic Club. He had sort of a throne in the basement. His building was very narrow and his medical offices were on the first floor. Down in the basement he had a Klan room, and he had a throne up there. When you went to see him about anything that wasn't medical, he took you down there and he got up on the throne and talked to you. I know that Dr. Rex and I were both young fellows and it was pretty embarrassing. We didn't get any place with him. Nobody else did, unless they had something he was for; if he was for it, they got anything they wanted. . . .

Locke set about to promote the Klan through partisan politics.

Denver's Mayor Ben Stapleton, a Klan ally, provided Locke with a secure base from which to work, but Locke had greater ambitions than simply controlling the state's major city—he wanted all of Colorado. Locke planned and organized for the 1924 election. On May 13, 1924, Klan leaders met in Denver from all over the state to mark the first anniversary of the Colorado Invisible Empire and to map their political strategy for the upcoming primary and general elections. Each county was assigned a Klan major, who appointed a captain for every block of six precincts. The major also selected three "emergency men" capable of managing any component of the county organizations. Down through the sergeants and corporals, the KKK organized, registered, persuaded, and plotted to get voters to the polls. The organization demanded strict discipline and a regular flow of information. Locke bragged that his plan was modeled "on those of the United States Army, where the command of a superior officer is never questioned."

Of the two major parties the Republicans proved more amenable to Klan influence. The Democrats strongly condemned the organization, cutting off any avenues for Locke in that direction. At this point, Morley enters the story as the Klan candidate for the gubernatorial nomination. This fifty-five-year-old Iowa native, a graduate of the University of Denver Law School, had joined the KKK and been elected Klokan, or investigator, for the Denver Klan. He made no secret of his affiliation. A mediocre law practice had been enlivened by his participation in Republican politics, which led to his election as district judge in 1918.

A weak, vacillating man, Morley had succumbed to Locke's almost hypnotic influence. A Morley statement, quoted in the *Denver Express*, February 20, 1926, showed the depth of the attachment:

> In times of trouble the Almighty always sends some men to lead us. God sent us George Washington when we needed a leader in our struggle with England. God sent us Abraham Lincoln to preserve the union. And God has sent us John Galen Locke to lead our city out of its terrible condition of chaos and trouble.

Meanwhile, Locke would not have his way without a struggle. Denver capitulated easily, and Fremont County fell quickly into line, but some of the other sections of the state held out against the Klan and its candidates. The group's coercive methods were demonstrated in Denver, where the Klan stationed police officers at the entrance to the Republican meeting with orders to deny entry to "anyone who is not a member of the Klan and except delegates, no one but Klansmen had tickets." Locke sat in the mayor's box at the rear of the auditorium orchestrating his triumph, and the Klansmen came through for him, giving seventy-five percent of their delegation to Morley and fifty-five percent to fellow Klansman Rice Means, candidate for the United States Senate.

The Republican State Convention met in Denver on August 6; the Klan, for all its efforts, held less than one-third of the delegates. Bested for top line designation on the ticket, Locke was still able to secure a place for his Klan candidates on the primary ballot; now it was up to the rank and file to decide. Both the Grand Dragon and the anti-Klan Republicans confidently predicted success in the September voting.

The small, bespectacled Morley openly paraded his loyalties. The *Denver Express*, August 8, quoted him at one Klan meeting, "Not for myself, mind you, do I wish to run, but for the benefit of the Klan." Sure of his Klan support, he moved vigorously to expand his Republican base by promising to cut government spending, tighten prohibition laws, and help farmers raise agricultural prices. He wisely hitched his campaign to Calvin Coolidge's presidential election bid. Morley may have tried to take the high road, but the Klan clung to its policy of playing rough politics. Members infiltrated an anti-Klan meeting in Denver and prevented the main speaker from talking; they sang "Onward Christian Soldiers" as he dejectedly surrendered and walked from the stage.

On primary day, September 9, the Klansmen placed "pink tickets" under the doors and mailboxes of their neighbors, listing every candidate and classifying each as "Protestant, Catholic or Jew." Unacceptable Protestant candidates merited a star next to their names, which meant "unsatisfactory because of Roman Catholic affiliations and friendships." Organization, dedication, emotionalism, and Democratic Klansmen crossing party lines to vote (primary laws permitted this) paid off—Morley, Means, and almost the entire Klan slate won. Locke's first goal had been achieved; the Klan had captured the Republican party, an apathetic majority falling victim to a determined minority. The course of the fall campaign was fixed.

The Democrats tried to make the Klan the issue in the fall election, a tactic which did them little good. The loyal, feisty *Durango Democrat* exemplified the approach:

> Morley, Means and Milliken [C.S. Milliken, candidate
> for Secretary of State] that triumvirate should spell it

115

Korley, Keans and Killiken, that klan bunch that would pollute a sewer. Vote the Democratic ticket.
[Oct. 7]

Means, Morley and Milliken on the Republican ticket have made splendid records as Ku Kluxers. Vote to destroy such cussedness in any party.
[Oct. 25]

The KKK-dominated Republican party kept its voters in line, and the Invisible Empire kept adding members. Together they forged an unbeatable combination. The election strategy was simple: support the national ticket and Coolidge, promote law and order, and uphold the "oldtime American virtues." It worked, as Klansmen swept all but four counties east of the Rocky Mountains and made strong inroads into the traditionally Democratic mountain and western plateau counties. Morley won the governorship; only two Democratic candidates for state office, both endorsed by the Klan, survived the Republican landslide.

Basking in this victory, Colorado Klansmen enjoyed another ego boost when Imperial Wizard Hiram Evans and several state Grand Dragons visited Denver, welcomed at the depot by Morley and Locke. A subsequent rally in south Denver drew a crowd estimated at 35,000.

Klan power rolled unrestrained, awaiting only the inauguration of its man to proclaim the millenium. Breaking every tradition, the inauguration was held in the Denver Auditorium. To a gallery of cheering KKK members, Morley outlined his backers' cure for Colorado's ills. He called for an end to coddling lawbreakers, advanced a plan to abolish state agencies (so he could reintroduce them and appoint new members, loyal Klansmen all), and, true to the faith, proposed legislation prohibiting use of sacramental wine. Applause greeted his every remark. Amid the Klan rhetoric were some ideas that sounded consistent with Colorado politics—assistance to help revive mining and funds for interstate river compact negotiations.

The fact that Klan power had reached its zenith as the speaker drew toward his conclusions went uncomprehended by his listeners. It was one thing to be on the outside looking in, quite another to sit in the seat of power.

Morley's first setback came within hours, when the new governor attempted to dismiss the National Guard Adjutant General and two aides on grounds of economy. They refused to vacate, and a district court later invalidated Morley's order.

The house and senate, in the meantime, received Morley's program. Its passage looked like a foregone conclusion with the overwhelmingly Republican legislature. Added to Morley's recommendations were bills advocated by individual Klansmen. The total package was largely predictable: abolish all state agencies except those created by the Constitution; strengthen prohibition enforcement; bar marriages between Orientals and whites; prohibit epileptics, drug addicts, drunkards, or persons charged with felonies from marrying; and repeal civil rights laws which guaranteed persons of all races and religions equal access to public accommodations. Altogether, 1,080 bills were introduced during the session. Not all measures, however, were punitive or prejudicial; the Klan backed a women's minimum wage and prohibition of child labor.

In the end, Morley, Locke, and their followers failed miserably, completely foiled in their attempts to understand and manipulate legislative procedures and power politics. In the house they managed to secure passage of some bills only by allying themselves with non-Klansmen loyal to the Republican party. In the senate the minority Democrats, skillfully led by Billy Adams, scuttled even that tactic by leaving bills stillborn in committee and using delaying procedures. Nine holdover Republicans, who owed nothing to the Klan's 1924 sweep, courageously refused to go along with the governor, and no administration promises, conferences, or threats could budge them.

Morley and the Invisible Empire employed punitive measures and incredible pressure against rebels. Senators who bolted were ostracized at the capitol and on the street. Every morning a copy of the unofficial KKK newspaper was laid on legislators' desks. It prominently displayed, front page center, a black-bordered "Roll of Dishonor" listing legislators who voted against "patriotic measures." Readers were urged never to forget those names.

When the legislature adjourned on April 15, 1925, eighty-five percent of the bills had gone nowhere. Only two Klan-endorsed measures became state law: schools were required to fly the American flag, and ownership or operation of a still became a felony. The Klan's prospects and programs lay in ruins. There was little Morley could do except take petty revenge here and there through appointments and other prerogatives, such as punishing Billy Adams by refusing to appropriate money for Adams State College in his home district.

Klan prestige and power died during that session; it had not been competently exercised. The trappings of office proved insufficient to guarantee success. Hostile legislators and bureaucrats thwarted the Klan at every turn, abetted by the outside pressure of a press and public growing ever more alarmed at the turn of events. At the moment of victory the war had been lost.

Morley proved to be exactly what he appeared to be earlier in his career, an inefficient, mean-spirited man. Locke was the real power, Morley his puppet. As Ben Poxson observed, "He didn't make up his own mind on anything; he did as he was told." In fact, the primary duty of one employee in the governor's office was to carry messages back and forth between the two.

The crusade having been lost, Governor Morley spent the rest of his term trying not to let state duties interfere with Klan obligations. He regularly went to Denver Klan meetings and always managed to have time to appear at the organization's special events. In 1926 he led a column of more than 500 men in a march down Sixteenth Street, where they stopped in front of a clothing store to demand dismissal of all employees lacking proper secret credentials. That meant employees not acceptable to the Klan, a most unusual demand by a Colorado governor.

Not all activities were Klan connected; at ceremonial functions Morley represented the state. When airplane service was opened linking Denver to Colorado Springs and Pueblo, he was there, along with Mayor Stapleton and other dignitaries. Two planes landed on that last day of May, the first in the morning from Cheyenne:

118

> ... on the crest of a zipping tailwind, a black-and-silver sky ship swung over Denver ... circled in a rapid sweep over Park Hill and skimmed to a perfect landing at the Don Hogan airdrome, East Twenty-sixth Avenue and Oneida Street. The 'maiden flight' of Colorado's own airmail fleet was history.

> [*Denver Post*, May 31, 1926]

The second plane landed that evening, the return flight from Colorado Springs:

> It was an epoch-making landing and hardly a person in the gigantic crowd estimated at from ten to forty thousand but realized they were seeing a new page written in Colorado history.

> [*Rocky Mountain News*, June 1, 1926]

The governor also declared August 1-3, 1926 as the semicentennial anniversary of Colorado and a state holiday. One might legitimately question how far Colorado had progressed in those years by comparing its governors and legislators. A none too flattering picture would emerge.

When possible, Morley honored the Klan. He made Locke an honorary colonel in the National Guard and assigned him as his own aide-de-camp. The two attended Coolidge's inauguration in Washington. Lesser Klansmen received gratuitous tidbits as well. In 1925, under a nearly forgotten anti-liquor law, Morley appointed prohibition agents, almost 200 by the end of the year. In that one sweeping gesture, he repaid campaign debts, found jobless Klansmen employment, and rewarded some of the Invisible Empire's leading local dignitaries. Fortunately, most of them did nothing; a few, however, took their obligations seriously and began raiding suspected bootleggers on flimsy evidence or without a warrant. Violations of constitutional rights generated a firestorm of statewide protest. Morley backed down on the year's last day and revoked the commissions. Not one to give up easily, he revived the idea in 1926, this time as nonsalaried, honorary positions.

The Klan era in the statehouse was over; two frustrating years had produced none of the expected blessings. Morley's sole contribution was a small surplus in the state treasury.

119

Morley's tragedy mirrored that of the people of Colorado who had elected him; for a brief time a vocal minority had wholeheartedly supported the Invisible Empire's bigotry and hatred. The Klan lost because its leaders lacked political astuteness and managed to blunder at almost every turn. Incidents of corruption among the leaders did nothing to enhance their law and order image. Morley's personal secretary was indicted for mail fraud; others were imprisoned for embezzlement and some for violating prohibition laws. Fortunately, Coloradans regained their senses and their perspective, as the hostile emotions of the previous years finally ran their course.

That Colorado survived this administration speaks well for on-going state government and, in a sense, the two-year term. Neither the state nor any individual gained from the experience, except in a negative way. With the 1925 failure of the Klan to pass its legislative program, its power eroded rapidly, hastened by charges of corruption, continued outside criticism, and mounting public revulsion. Locke soon stepped down under a storm of accusations (Morley stoutly defended his friend, to no avail); without this charismatic individual, the Klan had no future. In 1926 the Republican party cleared out its Klan elements and returned to its normal political ways.

The pathetic Morley left the state soon after his term expired and went to Indianapolis, Indiana. There, in 1935, he was indicted and later convicted of mail fraud; in 1937, at age sixty-eight, he was sentenced to five years in Leavenworth Federal Prison. Colorado had never seen his like before, and, it is to be hoped, never will again—nor the conditions that enabled him to win the governor's chair.

Colorado:
1930-1950

The depression meant not having a job, being unable to buy your child a nickel ice cream cone, losing your home for taxes, and seeing Hooverville shanties nestling next to depressed communities. It created as many memories as there were people. Eager to blame someone or something for this catastrophe, Americans found a scapegoat in the Republican party. The party had, after all, claimed as its achievement the "two-cars-in-every-garage" prosperity of the previous decade. Disenchantment with those promises swept the Democrats, Franklin Roosevelt, and a vaguely described New Deal into office in 1932.

Though vague about specific programs in '32, during the next eight years Coloradans learned all about the New Deal. The scrambled alphabet of New Deal agencies had more federal impact on the state than at any other time since the territorial days, when Washington guided the destiny of Colorado. When all was said and done, the New Deal had built libraries, hospitals, dormitories, campgrounds, dams, reservoirs, and roads, among a host of other things, and hired musicians, interviewed old-timers, taught the forgotten skill of gold panning, introduced farmers to new agricultural ideas, and built dioramas for the historical society. The money and ideas coming out of Washington tied Colorado to the federal government as never before in the twentieth century.

But the depression lingered, and not until the boom created by World War II did the state and nation finally shake off the effects of 1929. The war became a turning point in Colorado's history, as Coloradans again geared up for a war effort that would last for four long years. Denver was nicknamed the second Washington because of the number of federal agencies located there. Hundreds of thousands of service men and women passed through the state, a goodly number vowing to return to the mountains when the war ended. Then there were the 10th Mountain Division ski troops, who became some of the prime movers in promoting Colorado as "Ski Country, U.S.A." Aspen and Vail are two of the ski areas they managed to develop with outside help.

In the immediate postwar years Colorado lost the last vestiges of its frontier past and raced into the future. Population growth, suburbs, airplanes, skiing, tourism, uranium rushes, and television had entered the scene by 1950, as had the cold war, the higher education crunch, and a postwar baby boom. Colorado had crossed a watershed in its history; it would be impossible to return to the old days now. The future seemed as promising as at any time in the state's history.

Edwin Johnson. *Courtesy Colorado Historical Society.*

Conservative's Liberal: Edwin Johnson

... I was secretary to Governor Adams at that time. Ed came to Denver one day and came to the governor's office. And he said, 'Is it true that Billy isn't going to run any more? You'll probably know; the gossip is, he isn't.'

I said, 'As far as I know, Ed, he isn't going to run.'

'Well,' he said, 'does it make any difference if you serve out the rest of your term [as secretary] with the governor?'

'No, it doesn't make any difference,' I said.

Ed replied, 'Would you speak to the governor to see if he would appoint me as secretary if you quit, so I could get acquainted with all these people who come to the governor's office, because I want to run for governor.'

When he [Johnson] left the elevator [company], it went broke, you know, and he told me in this meeting where he talked about becoming secretary, that he lost $1200 in salary, which was a lot of money ... I never will forget that poor fellow sat there and the heels of his socks were worn clear up to here [pointing to his ankles] ....

In these words did Ben Poxson, secretary to Governor Billy Adams, remember one of those small incidents that altered Colorado history. It was 1931; Edwin C. Johnson—"Big Ed," as Colorado Democrats fondly called him—was Colorado's lieutenant governor, serving his first term after eight years in the state legislature. Proceeding cautiously, as

125

he was inclined to do throughout his life, he asked the attorney general, Clarence Ireland, for an opinion on the legality of this unique arrangement. Ireland ruled that Johnson could serve in both capacities, but would not be allowed to receive compensation from Governor Adams during the session of the legislature. Johnson thus filled both positions and laid the groundwork for his campaign for governor.

Even though the Republicans were reeling under accusations of causing the terrible 1929 crash and depression, Johnson would not have an easy time of it. His biggest hurdle lay within the Democratic party itself, the split between what might be called the rural and urban factions, in essence, Denver vs. most of the rest of the state. Representing the latter, Johnson had to face a primary, which he won, carrying even the capital city. He subsequently triumphed in November, running well ahead of the Democratic presidential nominee, Franklin D. Roosevelt. In 1932 and later on, his ability to attract votes proved impressive—Ed Johnson was popular with Colorado voters. The man who was called "the most discussed and often the most cussed Colorado politician" of recent decades now assumed a position of leadership that he would hold for nearly a quarter of a century.

It was January 1933, the depths of the great depression. Coloradans and "Big Ed" had never experienced hard times like these, although Johnson was certainly no stranger to setbacks. He had pulled himself up by his own bootstraps.

His parents were immigrants, and he had been born January 1, 1884 on a farm near Scandia, Kansas. "Big Ed" used to say that William Jennings Bryan was a substitute teacher at Lincoln High School, which he attended, and that Bryan's influence made him a Democrat (the rest of his family voted Republican). Graduating in 1903, he saw his chief ambition—to be a railroad man—thwarted by his youth and spindly frame. Instead, he became a train dispatcher, only to suffer another reversal when he contracted tuberculosis. In 1909 a doctor told Johnson he had only three months to live: "Go to Colorado; it's the only chance you've got." He did and it worked.

Six months in a tent colony and an indomitable spirit put this "lunger" on the road to recovery. He and his wife, whom he married in 1907, then homesteaded twenty-two miles west of Craig and one hundred miles from the nearest railroad, a formidable challenge on Colorado's last frontier. Homesteading meted out bushels of backbreaking work and few rewards. The young husband was forced to deliver freight and teach school to supplement his income. Defeat met his first attempt at elective office, that of Moffat County superintendent of schools. Disappointment came again when he was turned down for service in World War I.

The Johnsons had had enough of the homestead and moved into Craig, where he managed the Farmers Milling and Elevator Company. He expanded the business to include a small fleet of trucks to do hauling in the area, and he learned firsthand how painfully inadequate were the roads linking various parts of Colorado. The issue became a ready-made campaign platform for Craig's budding politician; politics soon took charge of his life. Before his retirement, Ed Johnson matured into the consummate Colorado politician of his generation.

After his 1914 defeat, he became a winner in 1918 when he was elected Moffat County assessor. Four years later, running on a platform of better roads, he won a seat in the state legislature, no small feat in strongly Republican, rural Colorado in the 1920s. Quickly attaining the rank of minority leader, the popular Johnson sought and won the lieutenant governorship in 1930, as Billy Adams secured his third term.

Now, in 1933, Johnson sat in the governor's chair. It was the 1890s all over again, only worse, and without the silver issue to distract attention from the unprecedented economic woes. The farmer, the merchant, the laborer, the teacher—no one was exempt from their impact. Hunger and unemployment threatened to unravel the fabric of Colorado's and the nation's government.

Colorado's public leaders and government stood helpless, unprepared to meet the crisis. Local relief, the first line of defense, was overwhelmed by the magnitude of need and collapsed despite heroic efforts. Private charities could not keep pace with worsening conditions. Self-help projects and cooperative ventures proved equally insufficient. Bitter protests demonstrated the unrest of angry, panicked people and sharply focused frustration on a system that appeared to have failed.

Bread lines, jobless transients swarming the streets, and people actually dying of starvation confronted Governor Johnson in Colorado and President Roosevelt in Washington in 1933. Their responses differed markedly. The president launched what became the New Deal, whose myriad agencies tinkered with, badgered, came to the aid of, and modernized America before running their course. The governor was concerned with a balanced budget and administrative reorganization. He asserted in 1934, "We need less of government rather than more and we need a curtailment and not an expansion of public service. At the rate we are going soon half of our people will be paid to regulate the other half." The New Deal and Ed Johnson were running on a collision course.

Johnson scored a success in the beginning, when he was able to consolidate some forty-four agencies into a five-man executive council. This long overdue overhaul of the state's archaic administrative equipment promised to end the wastefulness and inefficiency that had characterized Colorado government. The council, composed of department heads, gave the governor only five persons, instead of two score, with whom to contend. This progressive move improved some things but did not do all its backers had intended to expedite operations and upgrade the state's financial maneuverability.

Economy was the clarion call from the governor's chair and the legislative halls in '33. The "Local Government Budget Act" forced all governments, from counties to school districts, to initiate budgets. That word "economy," paired with tax reduction, was expected to be the magic elixir for depression-emaciated Colorado. Once the idea started to roll, it became propelled like a runaway express train. Why not consolidate counties in the name of economy in government? Thirty-six would be cheaper to administer than sixty-three; another report suggested they be melded into twenty-two. Johnson endorsed the idea of consolidation and then turned to a safe political ploy—he appointed a committee to study the plans.

When strong opposition blew up, he backed off. Economy was fine in its place, but not when it threatened the county seat, jobs, and political power. Natural sentiment and long-held loyalties for counties by their citizens had to be considered. The storm generated by the opposition rained its fire on Denver and had its effect: Colorado still has sixty-three counties.

Like other conservatives, Johnson attempted to balance the budget without increasing taxes, an impossibility during the depression. Colorado had been running deficits since 1931, and relief was desperately needed. The state had neither an income tax nor a sales tax to raise additional revenue, thereby handcuffing state officials, who might otherwise have initiated a large spending program to speed recovery. Ed Johnson's idea of what to do was expressed in a January 25, 1933 letter to a Denverite, Mrs. C.L. Laughlin, who as a last resort had turned to the governor for help:

> Your problem and the problem of tens of thousands of others in like situations cannot be met, according to my way of thinking, by charity. Our citizens want an opportunity to earn an honest living and they should have this opportunity.

> I am hopeful that the General Assembly will make it possible for the State to inaugurate a program of public work which will aid in alleviating the unemployment situation.

The legislature managed to sidestep the issue in the session starting in January 1933, taking the self-righteous position that any direct appropriation for relief must come from county and municipal governments, supplemented by federal emergency funds. Washington, however, was not that open-handed, unless the state was willing to contribute its share. It doled out money and waited for Colorado's matching funds.

Johnson was forced to call a special session in August, much against his will, to devise a tax. The outcome was a motor vehicle tax, with revenue earmarked for relief. This measure failed when a reactionary state supreme court struck it down as unconstitutional. The governor then summoned a second special session in December, setting a state record for one year. Unable to agree on a method to raise funds, the legislators adjourned for Christmas.

With no matching money forthcoming from the state, Harry Hopkins, head of the Federal Emergency Relief Administration, stated that as of January 1, 1934 all grants would be terminated. Alarmed at the prospect of losing federal funds, a group of irate depression victims staged a demonstration to pressure for action. The militants managed to scare some legislators out of their wits. They pushed their way into the senate, stampeding a herd of frightened legislators before them. Some called their actions a communist revolution, others a rebirth of the KKK, and a few calmer heads a protest against injustice by the unemployed. Whatever way the legislators saw it, they reacted by diverting highway funds to match FERA grants and imposed an excise tax on gasoline. A fraction of the proceeds from the tax was designated for relief and, by virtue of this action, federal contributions were assured.

If he could not beat the New Deal, Johnson would join it only kicking and screaming. His anger rose and the fight was on; he even went so far as to denounce the program as a fraud—strong words for a policy of his own party. Part of the problem lay in the personality clash between an over-achiever, activist, and professional social worker (Harry Hopkins) and the rural, conservative, somewhat rustic governor. "Big Ed" had run ahead of FDR in '32 and considered himself independent of any obligations to the party. He scorned federal relief programs as a waste of money and unwarranted interference in state and local affairs. These two strong-willed individuals were destined to clash, and a bitter four-year feud ensued.

Part of the controversy arose from the fact that Hopkins symbolized the corporate East and big government. Johnson doggedly opposed both as threats to his beloved Colorado. He wrote in 1939, "I think that Harry Hopkins did his work well but he was not responsible for the policy."

Johnson's humor was not improved when the liberal wing of the Colorado Democratic Party came out in support of Hopkins and the New Deal. He always encountered liberal opposition, partly because of his ties to Adams and other conservatives and partly because he did not embrace the Democratic and FDR agenda of the '30s. In 1934 one of Colorado's outstanding progressive women, Josephine Roche, challenged him openly for the governor's nomination. She was supported by Senator Edward Costigan, an early New Dealer and a Hopkins backer. Roche had attracted attention by allowing her Rocky Mountain Fuel Company to be unionized, and she paid higher wages than other Colorado coal mines. A friend of the United Mine Workers' John L. Lewis and a Roosevelt supporter, she could not have offered a more clear-cut choice between herself and Johnson.

Always the astute politician, Johnson played his cards masterfully. Just before the Democratic state assembly, the Highway Advisory Board completed its budget—4.6 million dollars in federal funds for highways. Johnson sat on the budget, subtly reminding the people that he had the power to change the budget recommendations and making it clear to the counties that a vote against him could mean the loss of highway funding. His ploy worked only in that the governor received top-line billing in the primary election he was forced to enter.

He won with 76,240 votes, but Roche still polled over 63,000. The vote gave clear evidence that not everyone in his own party went along with "Big Ed." Nevertheless, Johnson had a much easier time in the general election, losing only five counties.

The Hopkins/Johnson feud did not abate. To the governor, Hopkins was "full of theories on humane welfare of the parlor socialist type." The two men fought over appointment of FERA officials and the establishment of Works Progress Administration programs. Johnson won more battles than he lost in what might have seemed an unfair fight. His personal popularity and persuasiveness and his willingness to put all the necessary pressure on local welfare directors by threatening reduction of their authority turned the victory his way time and time again.

The highlight of Johnson's second term was his callout of the National Guard to prevent entry of migrant farm laborers in 1936. On April 18 fifty members of the guard were ordered to Colorado's southern border to repel the further invasion of "aliens, indigent persons or invaders." A states' rights man to the core, the governor did not hesitate in responding to labor's complaint that imported Mexican beet workers were depriving Coloradans of jobs. "Jobs in this state are for our citizens," he piously intoned and instructed guardsmen to refuse entry to the state to all non-Coloradans who had no reason to come in. Barricades went up; trains, buses, cars, and trucks were stopped and occupants questioned. Acting under martial law, the guard carried out what was popularly referred to as a "bum blockade." The *Durango Herald-Democrat* headline of April 20 was almost as blunt: "GOVERNOR CALLS OUT NATIONAL GUARD TO HALT INFLUX OF UNDESIRABLES INTO COLORADO."

The strategy did little except incite protests from both inside and out of the state and was soon stopped. The *Herald-Democrat* changed its editorial mind and blistered Johnson on May 2: "Governor Johnson's war with New Mexico having been abandoned, due to the fact that the Governor himself had become convinced of its plain damphoolishness, all that remains is for the taxpayers to pay the cost." New Mexico felt especially aggrieved that it had been treated as if it had some social disease.

Critics were amused by a story that one attractive Spanish-American woman was stopped and questioned about her financial status. Modestly turning away, she stunned the troopers by reaching into her stocking and producing a roll of bills totaling five thousand dollars. Pronounced desirable on the spot, she was allowed to proceed into the promised land.

Justifying himself, Johnson wrote the Reverend Edgar Wahlberg on May 4 that he had tried to work out an agreement with the governor of New Mexico, the railroads, and the beet industry. The latter two reneged on every agreement, "so I finally resorted to very drastic action." He went on to say, "I wish that you knew how these poor peons are brought in here and required to pay tribute to the racketeers who hire them out at so much a head with a rake-off on each person. Lincoln didn't free all the slaves in 1863. We have slavery in Colorado today competing with free labor."

Supporters of Johnson's policy, on the other hand, approved his motives in adopting this somewhat rough and direct tactic. They were less openly supportive of his actions. Individualism of that kind might once have been the hallmark of the west; in the face of the depression and the New Deal, it seemed out of step with the times.

Unswayed by the philosophical "nit picking," Johnson stayed on his conservative course. In April 1935 he vetoed a graduated income tax for Colorado, stating that income tax should be left to the federal government: "It would tend to scare investors from Colorado and cause an exodus of capital." He did succeed that year in persuading the legislature to accept a state bond issue for $15,000,000 to initiate a major paving program for the state highways. It was long overdue, as the former grain elevator manager well knew. In the end he could neither stop the rush of the New Deal nor slow increased federal and state involvement in individual lives. State powers were being eroded, despite his best efforts. He would rail bitterly and for years against the changing times and the New Deal. The *Rocky Mountain News*, October 25, 1944, quoted him as saying, "As I see it, the New Deal has been the worst fraud ever perpetrated on the American people."

During Johnson's years, Colorado had experienced a classic struggle between conservatives and liberals on the issues of federal vs. state power and welfare. Conservatism faltered under the demands of the poor and the depressed times but never fell. Johnson, backed by an apparent majority of Colorado voters, waged his campaign against the New Deal and Hopkins. In the end he left his successor (Teller Ammons) a one-million dollar deficit and a functioning, multi-faceted New Deal program in the state. Coloradans were eager to accept immediate, temporary help for relief and recovery and eventually sanctioned federal spending in the state. They agreed with their governor, however, that they wanted to have their cake and eat it too. Uncle Sam's rules, regulations, and involvement were something entirely different from programs, jobs, and financial assistance, in their opinion.

Johnson's Colorado career was far from over. In April 1936, Senator Costigan announced that he would not seek reelection because of ill health. "Big Ed" promptly announced for the seat, defeated his liberal Democratic primary opponent, and won in November. He was the only major office seeker in the United States who ran ahead of President Roosevelt in his reelection landslide. No one could doubt that he was the most popular man in the state.

A minor incident marred the last months of his term; microphones were secretly placed in the governor's office. Nothing was recorded, apparently, until Teller Ammons was inaugurated. Once the plot was uncovered, it turned out to be a 1937 tempest in a teapot; the press created an uproar in its attempts to uncover who and why. Transcripts were eventually published, but hindsight reveals the affair to be largely harmless with no serious ramifications.

Johnson was every bit the same maverick as a senator that he had been as governor. Various New Deal and Roosevelt programs came under fire from "Big Ed" as the years went by. An isolationist, he fought the United States' drift toward war right up to Pearl Harbor. He opposed Roosevelt's third term bid in 1940 and crossed party lines to support the Republican nominee, Wendell Willkie, and in 1944 broke with the administration and even Colorado Democrats. After the war, the old isolationist fervor lived on in his opposition to the Truman doctrine.

Colorado's senior senator occasionally played the buffoon. He sponsored legislation to establish a federal licensing system whereby Hollywood actors with questionable morals would not be permitted to act in movies. On the Senate floor, he denounced Ingrid Bergman for her affair with Roberto Rosselini and even proposed a Senate investigation into Hollywood moral standards.

All in all, though, he served his state well. In matters of water reclamation and regional development, farm and labor policy, and location of federal facilities, Ed Johnson was superb. After three terms, he announced that he would not be a candidate for reelection, but Coloradans would not let him quit. They wanted him to be governor again, so he accepted the nomination and campaigned by helicopter, a Colorado first. Winning easily, he served one more term as governor, 1955-1957. A few days after his seventy-third birthday, Ed C. Johnson retired. He had been in public office for thirty-four consecutive years, a record equaled by few other Colorado politicians.

Perhaps his long ago political opponent and longtime friend, the Reverend Edgar Wahlberg, best summarized Johnson's appeal and contributions in a 1983 letter to the authors:

> Colorado voters felt comfortable with 'Big Ed.' . . . Johnson may have fumbled and stumbled a bit. He never faltered. He worked hard. I never saw him lose his temper. There were times when he was disturbed. He was a Western individualist who boasted a bit about the real values. He loved Colorado—had some conflicts with neighboring states. He was shy about professionals. He finally agreed to appoint a Director for a State Department of Public Welfare. Instead of seeking a trained and experienced social worker he appointed a street car conductor in Pueblo. His judgment was good. This man fitted into the job with authority by reason of his ability. Johnson preferred down-to-earth people
>
> . . .
>
> There was a by-line in the thirties: 'If you want to vote for a conservative and a liberal at the same time vote for Johnson.' 'Big Ed' didn't mind this a bit. He thought it was 'horse sense.'

Ralph Carr. *Courtesy Colorado Historical Society.*

Forgotten Hero:
Ralph Carr

Colorado's governor's office, on the first floor of the State Capitol, is politically neutral. That is, it takes a temporary personality from its current occupant's pictures and mementos, but no individual governor is symbolized by the physical surroundings—with one exception: Ralph Carr. Just outside the office is a bronze plaque placed there by Japanese-Americans to honor a conservative Republican governor of Colorado, who in time of war-heated frenzy kept his head and the United States Constitution intact. He had the character and the courage to say no to hysteria. The plaque's dedication reads:

Ralph L. Carr
1887-1950

Governor of the State of Colorado 1939-1943

Dedicated to Governor Ralph L. Carr
a wise, humane man, not influenced by the hysteria and bigotry directed against the Japanese-Americans during World War II. By his humanitarian efforts no Colorado resident of Japanese ancestry was deprived of his basic freedoms, and when no others would accept the evacuated West Coast Japanese, except for confinement in internment camps, Governor Carr opened the doors and welcomed them to Colorado. The spirit of his deeds will live in the hearts of all true Americans.

Presented
October, 1974 by the Japanese Community and
the Oriental Culture Society of Colorado

137

This son of a hard-rock miner had traveled a long road from his birth in the now abandoned mining town of Rosita, Colorado on December 11, 1887. It had taken him to Aspen, Cripple Creek, and the University of Colorado, then back to Victor as a lawyer and manager of the *Victor Record*. He followed the same occupational pattern in Trinidad a few years later and in 1916 opened a law office in Antonito.

Carr served as a county attorney of Conejos County before moving to Denver to serve as Colorado assistant attorney general and then in 1929 as United States District Attorney. Like many another lawyer, politics attracted him; as a staunch Republican he found himself back in private practice in 1933 when the Democratic New Deal tide swept most Republicans aside.

Water and irrigation law became his specialties, a winning combination in the 1920s and 1930s as the various interstate water compacts were hammered out in conference and courtroom. During these years, Carr was a key man in many water development pacts agreed to between Colorado and surrounding states, and he served as legal advisor to the Colorado Interstate River Commissioner on the Rio Grande Compact in the late '20s and '30s. Throughout these discussions he strongly maintained and defended the position that the states had the right to administer and distribute the flow of western rivers. Carr's contributions and stand kept his name before both the Republican party leadership and Colorado voters, as did his work in criminal law. He was involved in some of the "big name" cases.

Despite protests that he did not want to run for the governorship, on the eve of the state convention his friends persuaded him to enter the race in 1938. "Rotund and volatile," a newspaper reporter dubbed him, he reportedly lost thirty-five pounds campaigning that year as he assailed "gross waste" in government and promised a "new financial deal" if elected. Carr won and became Colorado's first Republican governor in twelve years. Following his inauguration, he predicted that he would come to be the "most hated man in office." Outspoken and forceful, the new governor told newsmen, "regardless of what it does to me, I'll be governor in fact as well as name."

The *Salida Daily Mail*, January 10, 1939, commented, "Ralph Carr took over the reins of Colorado's administration at noon today and a half an hour later laid before the Legislature a concrete plan for balancing the budget, wiping out the seven-figure state deficit and paying a full $45 in old age pensions." His task was complicated by the fact that, as one person said, "the state was broke, I mean broke." The governor accomplished what he set out to do and in so doing incurred the wrath of many voters. He was criticized for releasing convicts, a "pardon and parole orgy" that aroused fears of a widespread crime wave. Carr labeled such allegations "silly" and later pardoned a number of people to serve in the armed forces. He remarked in his last state-of-the-state speech that of ninety-seven people he released to the armed forces, only four ran into problems. Although Carr never became the most hated man in office, as he had predicted, Coloradans always knew where he stood; he did not equivocate.

Their governor, courageous and independent, took stands on many state and national issues. He worked hard at "thwacking" the New Deal in Colorado, while at the same time backing Roosevelt's foreign policy going into the '40s.

An ardent supporter of the 1940 Republican presidential nominee, Wendell Willkie, Carr was rumored to be in line for a cabinet position. His friend Lowell Thomas contributed some "Carr for President" buttons. Neither possibility ever matured; Franklin Roosevelt won an unprecedented third term that year. Fortunately for himself, Carr had decided to stand for reelection, proclaiming that "every group benefitted" by his administration. His win set the stage for the confrontation on the Japanese-American issue. This situation evolved, not from anything the governor or the state did, but from "a date which will live in infamy," December 7, 1941. The Japanese attack on Pearl Harbor altered American history and proved to be a watershed for Colorado. The state never would be the same again, thanks to the developments which came along with World War II during the next four years.

This sudden, brutal attack angered and unified Americans as few other events have done in the twentieth century.

Governor Carr called for Coloradans to rally to the defense of "state and nation." In such a situation intolerance reared its ugly head against Japanese-Americans (victims of guilt by association) and aggravated fears of potential espionage and sabotage. Tempers flared almost overnight on the West Coast, abetted by a long-standing resentment toward these immigrants and unlucky American citizens. Newspaper, political, and public pressure mounted on Washington to take action. In 1942 over 110,000 Americans of Japanese descent were rounded up, primarily in California, and ticketed for evacuation far from the coast, where they were seen as a threat to the war effort. The only question was where to put the relocation camps.

Colorado and other Rocky Mountain states offered what seemed ideal choices, but resentment erupted even here. A *Denver Post* survey of some leading Denver businessmen and civic leaders in March 1942 indicated the feeling of many Coloradans: "Japanese aliens should be put in concentration camps; . . . under no circumstances should the Japanese be permitted to move about freely; . . . if it is necessary that they should be brought to Colorado, they should be under federal guard in our CCC camps (left over from Roosevelt's high tide New Deal days) and made to work on our roads." Federal District Judge Henry Hicks pulled no punches: "I am absolutely opposed to it unless all of those removed to this state are placed in concentration camps under Army guard. I am against humoring these people." United States Senator Edwin Johnson bitterly denounced bringing the Japanese to Colorado and favored laying the full responsibility and blame on the federal government if that should happen. Against this kind of fear and racist thinking, Ralph Carr took his stand.

If Colorado had stood alone with these attitudes, Carr might have been able to overwhelm the local opposition with pressure and rhetoric. Such was not the case. Other Rocky Mountain states reacted similarly, the general attitude being "Hell, no, if they're too dangerous for the West Coast, they're too dangerous for us." Billboards along highways said it all: "Japs keep going."

It took courage and a realization of what it could mean to one's political career to stand and be counted on this issue. Governor Carr did not mince words as he pleaded for unity:

> To the American-born citizens of Japanese parentage, we look for example and guidance. To those who have not been so fortunate as to have been born in this country, we offer the hand of friendship, secure in the knowledge that they will be as truly American as the rest of us. This is a difficult time for all Japanese-speaking people. We must work together for the preservation of our American system and the continuation of our theory of universal brotherhood.
> (*Las Animas Democrat*, April 3, 1942)

Pressure mounted on him to accept neither evacuees nor one of the relocation camps, but his opponents had not measured the man. He told a Boulder victory rally, "If I'm right, let's stop making threats against the Japanese. If I'm wrong you can oust me at the next election." Colorado's leading Democrat and best-known politician, Senator Ed Johnson, continued to disagree violently and openly criticized the governor's policy, as did many of the large Colorado newspapers. Virtually alone, the *Rocky Mountain News* stood by Carr.

The governor steadfastly persisted with his humane policies, trying all the while to modify the hysteria gripping the state: "An American citizen of Japanese descent has the same rights as any other citizen. . . . In Colorado, he'll have full protection." Unfortunately, as Japanese victory followed victory in 1942 and American defeat appeared to be a possibility, not many were in a mood to listen.

At a Salt Lake City meeting of western governors in early April, Colorado was the only state that offered to accept Japanese, should the Army decide to move them from the West Coast on a voluntary basis. The governors were almost universally opposed to the plan and agreed to admit them only if they remained under military guard. Carr alone made no objection to loyal Japanese-Americans moving into his state. In a *Denver Post* interview April 6 the governor explained why:

Coloradans must think intelligently about the war if it is to be won. We are at war and there are no state lines when we are at war. The President has established certain military zones, through executive order, within which certain people may not stay. He has put it up to the Army to enforce the order. The Army has said that certain people may be moved from these zones because it does not feel it is wise to take a chance on any of them. This is a war order to avoid fifth column activities on the West Coast.

I have been assured that there is no desire on the part of the government to bring Japanese into Colorado or any other states to compete with labor. It is simply a question of Americanism and patriotism. We are Americans and must do what the government desires to do. I have no right to question the wisdom of any order by a General of the United States Army while we are at war. Every state in the Union should be eager to comply with such orders while we are at war. This will be my policy as long as I am Governor of Colorado.

Some Coloradans rallied to support their governor, among them the Denver Ministerial Alliance. More typical were opposition groups, such as the Farmer's Union of Fort Morgan, which passed a resolution "absolutely against the transfer of . . . Japanese aliens on the West Coast to the beet growing section of the Rocky Mountain Region," and Greeley's city council, which voted unanimously to oppose any resettlement in its vicinity. One-hundred-sixty Swink residents demanded that the FBI stop any movement into their "unprotected" region.

Despite their concern, the fate of Coloradans in Greeley, Fort Morgan, Swink, and elsewhere did not lie in their own hands. Back in February President Roosevelt had signed the executive order to which Carr referred and had authorized the construction of "relocation" camps to house the Japanese. Now that the idea of voluntary resettlement had collapsed, the only question remaining was where the camp or camps might be situated in Colorado. Several towns, including Durango and Glenwood Springs, would have welcomed a camp, not necessarily from humanitarian motives, rather because of the business and profits to be derived. Rumors in April and May kept everyone on edge; Alamosa gained early favor to acquire a camp for 3,000 Japanese. Finally in May, Milton Eisenhower, head of the War Relocation Authority, asked Senator Johnson to submit a list of possible camp sites. The senator complied with fourteen prospects.

A site in the Arkansas Valley near the small town of Granada was eventually selected, and on a tract of 11,000 acres a camp named Amache was established. The camp's vanguard arrived in August. To people from the Pacific coast, August on the eastern Colorado plains must have been a rude shock and the coming winter a worse one still.

Meanwhile, protests against the relocation continued to rumble. Johnson had come up with the sites, but he made it clear that he still opposed the immigration and steadily denounced Carr. The American Legion urged that all Japanese aliens be placed in concentration camps for the duration of the war—and so it went. Carr held firm. He wrote to an official of the WRA when the first Japanese were being settled at Amache:

> States do not possess the power to pass on the admissability of Japanese evacuees from west coast areas. . . . No governor has the right to deny to any American citizen or to any person living within the country legally, the right to enter or to reside in or cross his state.

Cries of impeachment now were added to the din of opposition. At one point a threat of violence to these uprooted people arose from a southern Colorado town. Carr traveled to the community, confronted a mob, and gave them a stern warning, "If you harm them, you must harm me. I was brought up in a small town where I knew the shame and dishonor of race hatred. I grew to despise it because it threatened the happiness of you and you and you." The group disbanded, the threat passed.

Amache, named after the daughter of Chief One-Eye, a Southern Cheyenne killed at nearby Sand Creek in 1864, grew rapidly in the late summer and fall of '42. As best they could, the Japanese (two-thirds were American citizens) tried to establish a community with local government, school facilities, newspaper, library, YMCA, and even an American Legion Post. Water had to be hauled in from Granada when the local source proved to be impure. Irrigated acreage nearby produced melons, corn, and vegetables that improved the diet, as did hogs and chickens raised by the residents. Day-to-day living became easier in '43 and '44. The frightened, homesick families of the first months sank roots in eastern Colorado, and it was said that the instant city of Amache became the tenth largest in Colorado when it reached its full population of some 10,000. It closed in 1945, long after Ralph Carr had left the governor's office.

For the evacuees who suffered great economic loss (if not outright ruin), emotional turmoil, and personal shame, Carr's steadfastness generated one bright glimmer of respect. In the depths of their despair, the Japanese-Americans proved their loyalty and valor, from the homefront to the battlefield; Carr had been right. Among those who applauded Carr was *Time* magazine (September 21, 1942): "He proved his statesmanship and urbanity by his handling of the vexatious Japanese evacuation problem."

While the furor over resettlement heated to full blaze, Coloradans were preparing for an election year. It was rumored initially that Carr intended to run for a third term; he decided instead to oppose Ed Johnson for the United States Senate. A titanic battle erupted between the two stalwarts of that era's Colorado politics. They stood in opposition on the question of the Japanese-Americans, just one of many issues on which they disagreed. Carr ran hard and lost a close race.

It is difficult to evaluate the impact that Carr's stand on the issue of relocation may have played in his defeat. Reporter and writer Bill Hosokawa felt it "probably ruined Carr's political career." In the aftermath Carr himself blamed his defeat on it. In the final analysis, it appears that it must have swayed enough votes to insure Carr's defeat in a race as close as this one. In their own hearts, however, many

Coloradans undoubtedly supported their governor's act of conscience. Evidence of this was the landslide of negative public comments on Carr's policy compared to the narrowness of his loss. Silent support must have existed throughout the state.

Ralph Carr retired from politics after this and returned to his law practice. Elected and reelected a regent of the University of Colorado, he planned on making a statewide political comeback in 1950. He succeeded admirably, being nominated by the Republican party for governor, but he died suddenly in late September. Thus ended a full career dedicated to his native state.

Four individuals who described Ralph Carr concisely summarized his contributions and character. Ben Poxson knew him from the time the two of them were young men in the San Luis Valley and played on the same baseball team: "Ralph was a nice fellow, he was a grand fellow. . . . he was a real gentleman and one of the good governors, I would say, of Colorado." Judge Gene Breitenstein, his one-time law partner, observed, "His leadership saved the state from financial disaster and his Japanese-American stand brought honor and praise to the state. I feel that Carr did the right thing, the courageous thing, in permitting the location of the center down near Lamar."

In August 1976, at the dedication of a bust of Carr at Denver's Sakura Square, one speaker extolled the governor as one who "rolled up his sleeves on the side of the angels and helped the Japanese-Americans regain respectability." Perhaps Minoru Yasui said it best for all when he praised him as "one voice, a small voice but a strong voice."

Colorado: 1950-1976

If that nineteenth-century slogan "grow or die" had a ring of truth to it, then Colorado appeared as healthy as it ever had during the years after 1950. Its population was moving steadily upward, especially in the highly urbanized corridor along the foothills from Boulder to Colorado Springs. The front range counties came to dominate the state economically and politically as they never had before. The Supreme Court's decision of one man, one vote, which successfully broke the stranglehold the rural counties had held on legislatures here and elsewhere throughout the country, contributed to the political supremacy of these urban counties.

Denver became a metropolis of over 480,000 by 1976. When the totals of its suburban neighbors were added to that, it meant that half of all Coloradans were crowded into its capital city and the neighboring five counties. Denver had gone big time in other ways as well. Its symphony, for example, was becoming nationally recognized, its "brown cloud" infamous, and its entries into professional major league sports warranted television and sports page coverage.

While the front range boomed with investment, construction, and business, many of the other Colorado counties were still struggling to recover from the depression. The agricultural eastern plains steadily lost population, as did some of the mountain counties and the San Luis Valley. It was difficult to attract industries, doctors, and people to these areas where few jobs and other economic opportunities existed. Even the airplane and car did not relieve the isolation that some of these rural communities had endured for a hundred years. Colorado's diversity militated against easy answers to the question of how to reverse permanently the decline in the rural areas. Rural and urban Colorado had little in common, and mutual understanding remained hard to come by.

146

Instant communication and improved transportation removed the last remnants of isolation for the state as a whole. Coloradans were caught up in the immediacy of events in the twentieth century as they never had been in the nineteenth. They could watch the Vietnam war on the evening news and see live protest demonstrations after dinner. They suffered through Watergate and the energy crisis in the early 1970s like everyone else. All these things changed them, as did the environmental campaign from which the state had so much to gain or lose. Coloradans themselves were younger, better educated, and more affluent than their predecessors and these phenomena had a decided impact on state politics, an example being the 1972 referendum on the Winter Olympics.

The Centennial State attained its own centennial in 1976, with appropriate ceremonies and lots of fireworks. The frontier days of the 1870s lived on in tourist attractions; much of it seemed quaint to the newest Coloradans. Traditional ideas, such as growth, development, and progress, were being challenged and more concern for land and environment was being shown than ever before. Colorado, however, could not chart its destiny alone— Washington's policies and America's needs dictated state action in many cases. Colorado remained, even yet, an economic colony of outside financial interests.

Stephen McNichols. *Courtesy Denver Public Library Western History Department.*

"So Fleet the Works": Stephen McNichols

"I was born a block away from the Colorado governor's mansion and grew up at 607 Pennsylvania. I knew the block on the hill like the back of my hand. I used to take grapes and apples out of there many times as a kid." The speaker, Stephen McNichols, was referring to the house built by Walter Cheesman and owned after 1926 by Claude Boettcher. No individual deserves more credit for its becoming the governor's home than this one-time neighborhood boy who later became governor. Against advice from both political parties (a legislative committee voted ten to one to turn down the property) and friends, McNichols made the decision and accepted the house on December 30, 1959. Over objections that it was too big, too lavish, and potentially too expensive to maintain, he held firm. He also chose to ignore another concern—whether a Colorado governor should live like a millionaire. His lifelong attachment to the mansion and the neighborhood influenced his decision, as did the realization that it was "good business" and an important part of Colorado history.

This little episode tells much about the man, his administration, and his determination. Until this time governors lived in hotels, apartments, and homes of their own choice. This custom ended when the McNichols family moved into the mansion after seventeen months of painting, fumigating, and remodeling to make it "livable." Politically, the move proved to be a hot potato; the legislature dragged its feet on appropriations, and Republican criticism failed to subside until one of its own

149

entered it in 1963. Through all the furor, McNichols stuck doggedly to his plan. A July 1983 interview in the *Denver Post* found his position unchanged: "If I had the chance, I'd do it again. The Boettcher mansion was well-built, beautiful, and supplied with works of art and everything a state needed."

Seldom in Colorado history has a better prepared and politically experienced individual than McNichols assumed the office of governor. Forty-two years old in 1956, he had grown up in Colorado politics, his father having served as Denver's auditor for thirty years. A lawyer and veteran of the Second World War, McNichols was drawn into state politics, a natural leaning for this activist-minded Democrat. He won his first state senate race in 1948 and served through 1954, when he ran on the ticket with Ed Johnson and became lieutenant governor. In the senate he worked indefatigably for the establishment of a sound, long-range highway plan, a decades-overdue program in a state so dependent upon tourism.

As Ed Johnson's lieutenant governor, McNichols was presented with a rare opportunity. Johnson developed serious health problems and had to be hospitalized, giving McNichols the opportunity to play a substantial role in the day-to-day administration of state government. Fortunately, as he said, he had a good relationship with Big Ed, something not all party members could claim. "I regarded him as a friend, a very knowledgeable guy. But I was always trying to figure him out, because he would never let you figure him out, let you know what he was going to do." With a chuckle, he concluded, "He kept me on my toes all the time, but he was very decent to me."

Experienced in matters concerning the state and statehouse, and taking his campaign to the people, McNichols won his 1956 race to succeed Johnson. Even so, he was not an easy man for the voters to understand.

Reporter Tom Gavin, in the *Rocky Mountain News*, November 8, 1956, wrote that McNichols was a strange political animal, "a naturally reticent man who would just as soon envelop a stranger in a smile and a handshake." But he acknowledged him as a man of "ready wit and infectious laughter" and one whom "his enemies acknowledge" as a "fiery adversary."

He had campaigned on a well-thought-out program that included appointment of a committee for legislative reapportionment, a statewide watershed survey, the establishment of a state planning and public works agency, and a commission to study the Colorado tax system to recommend equitable apportionments. These ideas were not just campaign rhetoric; the governor had every intention of doing exactly what he had promised. The next two years, and the following four-year term (he was the first to win one), were spent trying to accomplish these plans and more.

His activism stirred up a hornet's nest of opposition, especially among the more conservative Republicans in the legislature. Not one to shrink from his expressed goals, McNichols pushed ahead.

> I was an advocate of what I believed. I never undercut anybody. I would tell them this is the way I feel about it, this is what I'm going to do. This is why I got in trouble with a lot of legislators who are always trying to trade something . . . I told them, look, if you don't like my program don't take it, I'm not going to trade you anything. I'll tell you what's wrong with what you're doing and how you can get me to support it . . . Once you start trading people things you're out of the capitol . . . They'll trade you out of the gold on the dome.

During that first term, an impressive number of things were accomplished.

Education was a pet project, and he strengthened the schools and other educational institutions with money and leadership. Under his urging—sometimes direct lobbying—the legislature adopted an improved school aid distribution formula. He also insisted on the reorganization of school districts; as a result, the number slowly declined. Concerned about higher education, McNichols was able to raise college and university faculty salaries by a median $1,200 a year, helping to stem the damaging flow of qualified professors from the state to industry and higher paying schools.

One of his great concerns was the state hospital for the mentally retarded and handicapped, which he found to be,

151

in his own words, a "snake pit—a mess." It took a terrific fight in Pueblo to bring the institution there into line and weed out the graft and incompetence. Buildings condemned years before still had people living in them. Whether Democrat or Republican, McNichols wanted the best qualified person to head the facility and the best possible program to help the inmates. The same was true of prison reform, long needed in Colorado. Looking backward from 1983, the ex-governor recalled with a grin, "I walked on a lot of toes and rolled things through. I never lost any major program; [maybe] it didn't come out exactly like I wanted, but I never lost any major programs."

To push his programs through, McNichols took risks and fought hard. The governor spent considerable time on the second floor of the Colorado capitol cajoling hesitant senators and representatives. McNichols reminisced about trying to find legislators who had voted against his programs and then undertaking to persuade them differently, going so far as to speak in the home bailiwicks of these people to incite public pressure. When necessary, he sought help from Republicans, particularly if he was being "blackmailed" by his own party or individual legislators in search of favors. Rather than dealing solely with Democratic party and floor leaders, he worked with the entire legislative delegation to avoid insulting anyone. This procedure naturally angered some of his party's leaders, who felt slighted by the governor's lack of attention.

Those leaders also objected to the fact that he sometimes turned to Republicans when he found himself in a tight spot and even voted for their program, "if a good one."

> When I had a good program I used to go down to the Republicans and say, 'Look, you know this is right, it's good; I've helped you on some things that are good. So I've lost some of my Democrats, and I'd lose them because I wouldn't trade them anything . . .

He laughed when he remembered that he encouraged some controversial legislators just to vote for his bill, not talk in defense of it and thereby possibly lose more votes. That was the political McNichols at his best—no risk, no gain.

152

Taking risks did cost him politically. Regardless, he moved to build up a state planning division with enough staff to operate successfully and "with nerve enough to say no." His budget office was highly praised. A reporter concluded during the 1958 campaign: "For the first time ever, Colorado's governor was able in 1958 to present a genuine executive budget to the legislature—a budget expertly analyzed, carefully pruned, but not butchered."

Nor did McNichols forget the highway projects dating back to his earlier legislative days. Colorado became one of the first states to receive its share of federal interstate highway funds, thanks to McNichols's interest and direction. And, finally, he pushed hard for a water resource study and cooperative water planning with the federal government. There was more, but the pattern emerges of a vigorous, activist executive willing to exert and endure pressure and to assume the risks of energetic leadership to achieve what was best for the state.

This was the same man who said earlier when sponsoring a constitutional amendment for a four-year term (passed in 1956): "You could never get anything done in two years, everybody was afraid to do anything. You know you can't do anything in two years, no program, no dynamic program of any kind. You've got to have four years to get it moving." He might have disproved his own forecast by what he accomplished in two years; nonetheless, Colorado voters approved his efforts and returned him to office.

Steve McNichols lost his reelection bid in 1962 to newcomer Republican John Love. Governor only six years, he was hailed for his gargantuan impact on Colorado's system of public policy. His list of accomplishments ranged over a wide area, including an improved highway program, a fair and equitable tax system, a campaign for a University of Colorado Medical Center, prison reform, and governmental reorganization. If one takes the position that government can play a positive role in the lives of people, few, if any, Colorado governors have accomplished as much as Stephen McNichols.

Why then, has McNichols been so largely forgotten within a generation, his multitude of programs scuttled, crippled, or incorporated into newer plans by succeeding administrations? From a philosophical viewpoint one might conclude that the voters and later political leaders were ungrateful. The reasons, however, lie with the man himself, partisan politics, the American political system, and Coloradans.

The genius of the American political system is that it provides for a bloodless revolution called an election every four years. The voters choose their leaders by ballots, not bullets. This system has served democratic countries, generally, and America, specifically, very well. On surveying the system, one has to marvel at the discretion of the voters, the resilience of America's political system, and its ability to find leaders in time of need. The downside of this system is that occasionally a good politician with all the right ideas will be thrown out of office for the wrong reasons. That trauma can scar the personality of the ousted politician. It is sometimes hard to be objective about not being reelected. It is hard to see the larger forces of democracy at work when a Winston Churchill is rejected in his hour of glory, or a Steve McNichols in his hour of accomplishment.

During the 1958 campaign Harmon Kallman, political writer for the *Denver Post*, analyzed the incumbent's strengths and weaknesses. He pointed out factors that hurt the governor. He had raised state income taxes and cut exemptions, both of which hit the taxpayer's sensitive pocket nerve during his second term. His water congress, which adopted a broad platform in June 1958, offered a good program, but it and the Fryingpan-Arkansas diversion project managed to set Western Slope and southeastern Colorado water interests at each other's throats, each stubbornly fighting to maintain its own rights. McNichols was criticized for being "power hungry," a charge that would not die. His use of power politics did not always reap rewards for the governor with the legislature or the public.

Kallman also felt that his acts of political courage harvested a mixed crop. It might be a courageous and necessary reform to rally a once-complacent State Board of Equalization to order a property tax boost for improving education, but taxpayers too often are unforgiving of tax increases at the next election, regardless of the reason. In 1962, when the Republicans promised much and ran an Eisenhower look-alike candidate who talked of reducing taxes and curbing Colorado government, the electors remembered those taxes. In the years that followed, for better or worse, they followed the same course, and McNichols's hard-won programs evaporated or were changed beyond the original intent.

The risk-taker had taken the risk, lobbied his programs through, and stepped on sensitive toes in and out of his party. He felt that for the sake of human justice and economic development it was necessary to take on a large number of governmental crusades with near-messianic fervor. Coloradans did not always understand the implications and need for his programs. Perhaps he was a prophet ahead of his time and, in some ways, without honor in his own state.

Coloradans proved a transitory lot in the McNichols years and afterward. Consequently, it was not long before a large group of new voters was totally unfamiliar with what the ex-governor had done or tried to do during his administration. Then, too, his aggressiveness seemed more like abrasiveness to some. They had no intention of fondly remembering or honoring him.

Despite having advocated needed programs and pushed them through, McNichols faded from memory, joining his less illustrious predecessors as one of Colorado's host of unremembered governors. The once-familiar words on the curtain of Denver's Tabor Grand Opera House come to mind: "So fleet the works of men, back to the earth again; Ancient and Holy things fade like a dream."

Asked to evaluate his contributions, McNichols forcefully stated without a moment's hesitation:

> Things that I advocated, the things that I recommended, were not small things—they were dynamic things, things that really affected this state . . . I think the mental health program was probably my greatest satisfaction . . . doing something for those hospitals, retarded children, and the $20 million

medical center. Very worthwhile things. I was very proud of the tax program, because I think it was done fairly and equitably. I think it spread the tax load the way it ought to be spread. Not perfect, but it was equitable. The highway program is a great source of accomplishment to me, because it was such a tough battle.

The battler in him has not given up. It was almost as if he were once more advocating his programs to reluctant legislators and a skeptical public.

The governorship during McNichols's era operated through a transitional period between the old and new, reflecting the state's situation. The easygoing days of the nineteenth century had vanished long ago, and the days of the 1920s and the depression '30s seemed almost as antique. The public now was demanding a new leadership role and fresh perspectives from the governor, along with some of the traditional patterns. No matter what his qualifications, so much depended on the personality of the man in the office. It could be trying for the governor. McNichols explained:

Well, there was an immense amount of things that you had to go to . . . rodeos, etc. Fantastic waste of your time, not a waste of your time exactly, but to have to go to everything! If you go to one county you have to go to the other. You have to spread yourself around. People expect an awful lot more from you than they ought to in terms of where you go and when you go. Some of those things are important. But God!

Then there were the hard choices that had to be made, especially over the ever-increasing complications of taxation and water. Colorado at the time was becoming more urbanized, with the population, economic power, and water needs concentrated along the front range. The Colorado legislature, however, came nowhere near to accommodating these changes; it remained rural-dominated and its majority often did not have the experience or temperament to comprehend or understand completely the changes taking place. These things only added to the frustration of a governor like Steve McNichols.

156

Reminiscing about his administration, McNichols discussed what he considered his toughest decisions:

> The ones that affected me the most, I think, were the death sentences. God! Letting somebody die was really tough. Somebody's mother would come up there—the kid's got a record as long as your arm, her life's devoted to him . . . she comes up and asks you 'you going to let my son die?' . . . that's the thing that bothered me the most.

Although one might picture governors working only on legislative matters, developing programs, and taking part in ceremonial functions, the job also has its individual moments of sadness and joy. Those stay with the man long after his term has ended.

Recalling his two terms, Steve McNichols had no regrets:

> I'm sure I made a lot of mistakes, but just looking back at it on balance and looking at it in the theories and thrusts of the things I was trying to do and what needed to be done at the time, I think I would do it again. Even though I lost, losing an election is not the worst thing in the world that could happen to you. Right? So what, I'm satisfied.

He did display a tinge of bitterness about the fact that the next governor, the Republicans, and the legislature let things drift after he left office; they "made one decision—not to decide."

157

John Love. *Courtesy* Durango Herald.

A Man for His Time:
John Love

The car lights cut through the cold, dark evening, illuminating the ribbon of Highway I-25 as it stretched between Colorado Springs and Denver. It was election night, November 6, 1962. Down the highway came a limousine, rented from the Broadmoor Hotel, carrying John and Ann Love, their children, and their good friends the Harrie Harts. Alternately triumphant and introspective, they listened to the radio's election returns as county after county reported an increasing lead for Love over the Democratic incumbent, Governor Steve McNichols. The trend had been obvious earlier, almost from the time they first heard the initial scattered precinct returns while eating dinner at the Cheyenne Mountain Country Club. John A. Love, age 45, was going to be Colorado's next governor; the good news sent them on their way to Denver with pride in the victory and awed by the responsibility descending on them.

As the Loves sped toward the Denver victory celebrations, they contemplated his meteoric rise from Colorado Springs lawyer, who had never held an elective political office, to governor-elect. Despite the optimism of the closing days of the campaign, an aura of disbelief affected the car's passengers when they considered how far he had climbed in so short a time.

Born November 29, 1916 on a farm near Gibson City, Illinois, he had moved to Colorado Springs when four because of his father's lung problems. Like some of the governors before him, Love and his family had been

159

attracted to Colorado by its healthful climate. Unlike some of their predecessors, however, the Loves did not venture blindly to a new land; the father had lived here briefly in his youth. An aunt and John's grandmother still lived in Colorado Springs, waiting to welcome them. After graduating from Cheyenne Mountain School in 1934, Love enrolled at Denver University, earning his room and board by working at Denver General Hospital, where he became adept at washing dishes and peeling potatoes. He found time to involve himself in campus activities, particularly the student newspaper, *The Clarion*, of which he became editor in his senior year. He was also elected president of the Rocky Mountain Collegiate Press Association. Following graduation, Love entered the DU Law School, receiving his LLB in 1941 and passing the State Bar the same year. As it did to so many other Americans, World War II interrupted the start of his career when he enlisted in the Navy's Aviation Cadet program; he won his wings and commission at Corpus Christi, Texas, on October 23, 1942, the same day he was married.

After the war, Denver first was weighed as a potential site for launching his legal career, but the scant availability of offices, housing, and homes fit for an untested lawyer's pocketbook forced Love to go elsewhere. So he moved on to Colorado Springs, into a home owned by his wife's father, and rented office space with a local attorney.

All these events seemed like ancient history on this November evening. In the years that followed his move to Colorado Springs, Love had traveled a path familiar to lawyers, one that led directly into public life. Early in his legal career, perhaps even as far back as high school, his goal was to become active in the public arena at some point. "I still wanted to become active in public life, but I felt that it was a poor activity if you had to rely on it for your living." There the matter rested while he developed his law practice. Finally, in 1962, John Love made his decision: "I looked at myself in the mirror . . . and realized that time was passing by and if ever I was going to do it, why I'd best get at it." Ironically, a few months before making this momentous decision, he had been defeated by one vote in his race for El Paso County Republican chairman.

The erstwhile candidate then weighed the political realities:

> My first idea had been, in years gone by, to run for Congress . . . but it was a seat held by a man, Judge [J. Edgar] Chenoweth, who had been there a long time and gave no evidence of retiring. The gubernatorial situation seemed to me to be wide open that year, and I felt, to begin with, that even if I were not successful, that it wouldn't be a minus insofar as running for something else again. It would give me experience, a name awareness, and so on.

What happened next was in a way amazing and reflected the political climate of Colorado during that era. With Colorado and state politics in transition and the Democrats and Governor McNichols in trouble, it was a propitious time for a political newcomer to venture forth. Love had first to win a primary battle against a longtime legislator and Speaker of the House, David Hamil. His friend and state senator from Colorado Springs, Harrie Hart, agreed to sign on as campaign manager.

Even though he had chosen a good time to run, it still took courage for this political novice to jump into the race. Never particularly active in the party in Colorado Springs, nor involved in the community beyond the chamber of commerce, and without much political experience, Love had no strong natural base or supporting voting bloc. "There is audacity there—it is breathtaking," commented Richard Lamm as the two men discussed Love's political rise. Both laughed, and Love went on to describe how the political ball began rolling in early 1962: "I mentioned in Montrose that I was considering it, that's the first press I had on it." Laughing again, he recalled, "I remember one of the first political speeches I ever made was up in Leadville on Lincoln Day, a lousy speech."

After that experience, one of his friends realized that such an image and style could not win and hired a speech coach for the would-be candidate. The three of them spent a weekend isolated in a winterized cabin near Leadville, where Love was coached on how to make a speech. The pupil proved apt, the "training" paid dividends, and the campaign trail was resumed.

Love and Hart took to the road.

> We had a car one of the dealers had let us have for the campaign, and we simply started in an orderly way and traveled the state, went to every not only county seat but other towns, called the party people and hopefully went on the local radio and later walked the streets and shook hands. But to begin with, the first tour around we spent a lot of time just driving the state, primarily (to) call on those people who were apt to be delegates.

With no political record to defend and no enemies eager to press old grievances, Love proved to be the right man at the right time. In many ways he was to Colorado what Dwight Eisenhower was to the United States—a thoroughly appealing candidate. Picking up support from the party leaders and from the rank and file, he won top-line designation at the state convention and went on to win the primary.

Fortune smiled, and Love himself admitted that "the timing, just everything was right." The articulate, handsome candidate took his campaign throughout the state, backed by a unified Republican party, though he had no cause or program to promote. Where he did not go, his effective advertising and eager workers kept his name prominently displayed. All these fortunate circumstances conspired to put him on the road to Denver that night of November 6, 1962, heading toward victory parties and, in January, the governor's chair.

There may not have been anyone better suited to govern Colorado in the early '60s. The state and its residents were undergoing changes and looked to new leaders unfettered by old issues, tired answers, and party ties. Like some other candidates, Love seemed to rise above and to separate from party affiliation; he was young and from an urban area, both traits more and more typical of Coloradans.

In 1959 Colorado celebrated the centennial of the Pike's Peak gold rush and, two years later, that of its territorial

162

status. The changes of the pioneer days paled before those of the 1960s. Ever since World War II the state had been growing and generally booming. Those two decades had transformed the face of Colorado. The old war-horses, mining and agriculture, now played less significant roles in an increasingly urbanized, industrialized, and tourist-oriented state. Add to these developments a great infusion of federal funds and workers, from national parks to military bases to Denver's multiplying government agencies, and it was obvious that the economic base had diversified. Nicknamed the "second national capital," Denver was a mushrooming city on the verge of becoming a large metropolitan complex with all the attendant problems. Wielding even more power than it had a century before, Denver correspondingly generated more fear and jealousy throughout the state. Animosity was particularly aroused when Denver cast covetous eyes on Western Slope water. This was the Colorado John Love confronted during his first term.

Gilpin, Routt, Adams, and Waite would have been confounded by the complexities of the job. Love described his schedule:

> The most important thing you have is your time . . . you have to have one person who is in charge of the schedule—you can't let it be fragmented—who keeps the book that puts people on or off the schedule and keeps it moving too. And I think that was one of the greatest adjustments I had to make was to learn to live with that kind of schedule. I didn't seriously do anything that wasn't on the schedule. That is a joke that my wife or children felt that they almost had to get on the schedule to get something done, because in addition to the governmental work there is a tremendous amount of ceremonial. That is, appearances, speeches, whatever it may be. Every organization in Colorado feels that if they are going to have a meeting then the governor should be there.

The governor was on call day in and day out in Colorado and more and more for obligations outside the state.

Though accused of overseeing a "caretaker" administration similar to Eisenhower's, Love presided over a state painfully examining its programs and expectations. The whole country was experiencing the same trauma.

Unrest in the cities, minority demands for long-denied rights, ever more violent protests against America's military involvement in Vietnam, the youth revolt, and other headline-grabbing incidents filled the television screen and newspaper pages. Even mountain-protected Colorado was lashed by the winds of change, though the effects were not so dramatic as elsewhere: "I feel pretty proud of the fact that in a period that nationwide was filled with a good deal of upset and violence that we did manage Colorado, I think partly through my efforts to maintain an equilibrium."

Confrontation did come to Colorado, however; the newspapers called it "Woodstock West." Some "hippies"— the "rock kind of people"—camped in temporary quarters they built on the University of Denver campus. University and local authorities failed in efforts to move them and finally called on the state for help. Fresh in many minds was a recent similar situation at Kent State in Ohio, which led to bloodshed and death. Governor Love met with the "kids," to no avail. "I wonder again at my audacity. I called out the guard . . . we attacked at dawn, but we had no bullets in the guns, and there was certainly no secret because there were enough kids out there that were members of the guard." The incident ended on an upbeat note; as Love explained, "we came and they were all gone."

Assessing his role in these difficult times, Love analyzed the governor's power and ability to change things:

> When it comes down to the specifics in instituting a program or fiscal policy, or whatever it may be, you come ultimately to this problem of the separation of powers in the legislative and executive. And the governor does not have power, nor should he have the power, to direct the legislative branch. It's a matter of leadership and persuasion, and I think that I was successful in most of the programs that I sought to institute. In the budget, they were always a little more conservative than I wanted to be, but I don't think

that's a bad system, that kind of competition that does exist.

Signs were already appearing that the legislature planned to play a larger role in budgetary matters. Love felt that his "biggest problems were always budgetary." Even in these years, the governor and the joint budget committee squared off, seeking to acquire or retain power. "It [power struggle is not a good thing to have," the ex-governor said in 1983.

> They would do the kind of things that you [Lamm] are plagued with, start putting in the footnotes and attempting to have a hand on the till of what I think should be executive administrative kind of duties and responsibilities. And I started out as you know, vetoed a great many of them. Got away with it, I think, the first time, but then I finally got sued on it . . .

That financial relationship between the governor and the legislature has not improved in the years since then.

John Love was particularly proud of his work in education, believing it to be one of the most important issues during his years as governor. Postwar America and Colorado relied on education, particularly higher education, to prepare their citizens to cope with a steadily shrinking, complex world. Colleges and universities in the state increased in number and size as never before, which required money, planning, and a willingness to recognize problems.

> The general goal and philosophy I had is that we wanted in Colorado to provide a system whereby every Colorado high school graduate who was so motivated could go on to college or university education. At the same time, it seemed to me that college administrators, being human, tended to be something of empire builders, competitive with each other. They would want to have their particular institution grow at a greater rate and have a higher salary for their faculty and so on. It wasn't only the administrators . . . much of the push behind that kind of attitude comes from the local chamber of commerce type of feeling. That is, Greeley wants the school to be a university, and Fort

Collins wants CSU to be as good or better or bigger than the University of Colorado, and so on down the line. . . . So the effort had to be made in an attempt to bring an overall rational kind of approach, a plan to it. This attempt is made through the commission on higher education.

Educational support did not guarantee freedom from criticism, especially when the matter of tuition was involved. During his first term, tight economic times created a budget crunch in Colorado. The "rookie" governor advocated raising tuition, "charging those students who could afford it a more reasonable [realistic] price for their higher education." It was, he confessed, "a naive thing to do politically. I got hung in effigy on campuses." John Love was learning the facts of political life from the governor's chair, a place usually reserved for political "pros."

Love learned his political lessons and won second and third terms by projecting an image of evenhandedness, stability, and fairness. Commenting on the image issue, he called attention to something that was becoming increasingly crucial in the media-oriented world: "you have to convey the image and have it believable that not only you personally are honest, but the government, its system, is fair and honest—to get the belief and the credibility." Speaking with Governor Lamm, he added, "I think I told you one time, I think it's true that one of the governor's jobs, whether he wants it or not, in addition to being governor, is to a certain extent high priest." One could speculate on what Routt, Peabody, or Johnson would have thought of the new image.

With regard to the Republican political spectrum, Love placed himself in the "progressive," or moderate, wing of the party, the Teddy Roosevelt branch. He displayed progressive leanings in his State of the State messages in 1970 and 1972, when he stressed the necessity for increased action to "preserve, protect and improve our environment," the long overdue need for statewide land use legislation, and a concern about growth simply for growth's sake. These ideas, heresy to the more conservative members of his own party, had become of increasing concern to many

166

Coloradans. The environmental movement of the '60s picked up momentum. Few environmentalists in the United States had a finer quality of life to preserve and maintain than those in Colorado; conversely, few were faced with losing more.

Even the best of intentions, however, can run afoul of emotions and reality, as the governor found out. Back in the late 1960s Colorado leaders had begun to consider the possibility of providing the site for the 1976 Winter Olympics. No one more sincerely wanted to win that bid than John Love. As he emphasized in a January 1970 message, "all Colorado" should approach with pride the opportunity to host the Olympics: "We shall provide the best facilities and the best games ever." Unfortunately, the backers sorely misunderstood the new concerns of Coloradans. The proposal incited an uproar that gave rise to an initiated amendment in 1972, which ended all hopes for the Olympics by refusing to allow state money to be spent on financing the games. Coloradans had clearly become skeptical of the old "Sell Colorado" theme; a fresh approach would have to be found. It was a personal frustration for Love, who had worked diligently to gain the Olympics and defeat the amendment.

Perhaps it influenced a decision he made the next year. In July 1973 he resigned to become director of the Office of Energy Policy for the ill-fated, Watergate-logged Nixon administration. Reviewing that fateful choice, Love [responding to a question about whom he had consulted before accepting the job] said in a sad voice:

> Well, I hesitate to confess that I didn't consult much of anybody. As a matter of fact, I didn't consult even with my wife, and I have since rued and regretted that. . . . And Al Hague again called on this oil or energy job, and I think that that job looked big enough to me to warrant the kind of wrench and gamble.

That was it, ten and a half years as governor at an end. Love moved on to Washington and a different challenge. A few months later, as the Nixon administration hurtled toward collapse, he resigned and returned to Denver.

Love had achieved much and been involved in myriad issues during his three terms. On being asked what his accomplishments were, he concluded:

> Oh, I think I have to get fairly general. It seems to me that . . . a good many things set the ground work and also started what I think of as modern Colorado, the growth and the high tech and the ski areas, and so on. In addition to that, I think that perhaps I made a substantial contribution in simply presiding and leading in a very difficult time in a way that saved Colorado from as much division as much of the rest of the country had. I think we handled the problems on the campuses and the racial problems and so on . . . , and I think that I, with my relationship with minority groups and with people generally, made quite a contribution in keeping Colorado on an even track.

Love could claim his share of success, and he had to accept some setbacks. Governors who followed could well appreciate many of the issues and problems that were just emerging during these years.

What evaluation can be made of John Love and his administration from the recent vantage point of the 1980s? Perhaps Republican stalwart and legislator Ron Strahle said it best: "He governed Colorado with stature and class at a time when those qualities were most needed."

Epilogue:
A Day in the Life
of a Governor

There is no such thing as a "typical" day in the life of a Colorado governor. The era under discussion, the issues of the day, and the personality of the office have shaped his schedule. It is possible, however, to give the reader some sense of the hectic pace, the myriad issues that bombard a governor daily.

Ben Poxson, secretary to Governor William "Billy" Adams, remembered his schedule. Adams served three terms, 1927-1933, a time that seems more removed from the present than the fifty years it is. "The Governor," Poxson wrote, "was an early riser and also showed up at his office even before the arrival of the janitor." Adams's day started at 6:30 a.m. and ended at 6:00 p.m.

6:30 a.m.—Breakfasted at the Brown Palace, which was also his residence while in Denver from the day the hotel was built until he retired as governor.

7:30 a.m.—Arrived at his office in the capitol.

7:30-9:30 a.m.—Reviewed previous day's conferences and took care of previous day's requests from state officials and the public.

9:30-10:00 a.m.—Press conference.

10:00 a.m.-12 noon—Met with state officials having official business with governor.

12:00 noon-1:30 p.m.—Lunch

1:30-3:30 p.m.—Met with the public (appointment not required, public encouraged to call).

3:30-4:00 p.m.—Press conference.

4:00-6:00 p.m.—Took care of daily correspondence and delayed state business affairs.

6:00 p.m.-Evening Hours—Evening social engagements delegated to subordinates.

The pace has changed in the 1980s. As this composite day demonstrates, it is somewhat like trying to drink from a fire hydrant. The pressure and volume of problems exceed the time available. Each day entails hundreds or even thousands of judgments and decisions that can come back to haunt one. Governor Richard Lamm recalls one of his days.

Up at 6:00 a.m. to read the state's two largest newspapers and to sign some mail while watching the early morning news.

7:30 a.m.—Breakfast with key legislators and staff members at the mansion to discuss some problem that has arisen. Schedules are usually made out six weeks in advance and breakfasts are often the only time available for a late-breaking issue or emergency.

8:30 a.m.—Security officers arrive and you leave for the Capitol, reviewing the schedule for the day and reading the background memos for the first meeting scheduled at 9:00 a.m.

8:45-9:00 a.m.—In the office. Place a couple of calls to Washington, D.C., to take advantage of the two-hour time difference. While waiting for the calls to go through, review the requests for staff time that have accumulated since the office opened at eight. In the fifteen minutes before your first appointment, you also dictate a couple of thank you notes from the previous day's activities, see your chief natural resources aide about a wilderness issue, and take one of the Washington calls which has been returned.

9:05 a.m.—The first meeting commences with a Chamber of Commerce delegation that wants to discuss a pending legislative package. In the thirty seconds before you tell your secretary to "show them in," you run your eyes down the list of their names to make sure that you will be able to recognize as many as possible. Meet around the large meeting table in the governor's office. Halfway through the 9:00 meeting, one of your congressional delegation calls, so you excuse yourself, walk over to the desk to take the phone call, and explain to the waiting group that one policy you must have is always to interrupt a meeting for a U.S. representative or senator. Taking notes on a yellow pad, one of the five yellow legal pages you juggle through the day, you remind yourself to talk to your appointments secretary about a candidate for the Colorado Advanced Technology Institute board and also to send a note congratulating a corporate executive on a forthcoming retirement. Two issues with the Chamber of Commerce can be solved immediately. A third one has to be worked out with a department head. The fourth proposal demands further thought and you tell the delegation that you are in agreement on two of the issues, the third is to be worked out with the Executive Director of the Department of Labor and Employment, and you will get back to them on the fourth issue. As you are seeing the delegation out the door, your secretary hands you four letters that have to be signed "before noon" and you sign these letters while the next group is coming in.

9:30 a.m.—Staff meeting to discuss a fiscal crisis, but before the meeting is really able to commence, you scan three telegrams that have arrived and telephone your wife at home to remind her your tuxedo needs to go to the cleaner before next Saturday night.

The meeting on the budgetary crisis begins with cabinet and staff reports, but in the middle of the meeting you realize that a key fact is not available. One aide goes out to phone to get the fact. You ask your secretary to return another call to Washington while you continue your quick survey of the morning mail. The aide comes back in, the fiscal crisis is further discussed, a strategy is agreed upon, and you agree with your legislative liaison on a message to the legislative leadership on the tentative resolution. At ten o'clock you slip into the little restroom aside the governor's office to comb your hair and get ready for the next quick series of ceremonial appointments.

10:00 a.m.—You kick off United Way Week with a proclamation, pose for pictures with Miss Teenage Colorado, and reenact a bill signing for a couple of legislators who need the photo for their local newspapers. Of the six people who have passed through your office, three have stopped to buttonhole you about unrelated problems, requests, or invitations. The invitations go immediately to the appointment secretary; the problems are assigned to an aide, and the request is solved by giving the person a Colorado pin. While the next group is being ushered in, the phone rings, so you ask the other people to hold at the door while you return a call from the Secretary of Labor in Washington on a peculiar problem with the Job Training Partnership Act. The next group comes in for a picture promoting the Cancer Crusade. Light bulbs flash and you blink three or four times to clear your eyes as the next group, proclaiming it Aviation Week in Colorado, comes in the door. DeMolay is followed in turn by the Daughters of the American Revolution and at 10:40, ten minutes after the scheduled half hour, the last of the guests are ushered out and the press secretary comes in with a reporter who wants to interview you about water in the West.

10:40-11:05 a.m.—This is the interview on water in the West, followed by a one-minute taping of a public service announcement calling attention to Drug Awareness Week. Before your 11:00 meeting commences, two aides come in for quick consultations. One needs to know whether a department head should be invited to a particular meeting; the other seeks last-minute guidance on the Rotary speech you are giving at noon.

11:00 a.m.—A delegation of legislators, along with their local hospital administrator, comes in to describe how unfair the Colorado Certificate of Need process is to their local hospital's expansion and to request you to "get involved" with the issue to stop wasting time and money. During the meeting you remember that it's one of your children's birthdays tomorrow and you make yourself a note to stop by a sporting goods store on the way home from work. Tell the hospital delegation that you very much believe in using the regulatory process to keep hospital costs under control, but sympathize with their need for a fast answer. You'll ask the agency head to give them an expeditious answer, yes or no. At the end of the meeting, one of the legislators stays over to ask if a local mayor can be appointed to a particular board and if the governor can quickly step out to have a picture taken with a hometown constituent who is waiting in the outer office.

11:35 a.m.—A phone call comes in from the head of Corrections with word of a possible prison disturbance later that day. At the same time the press secretary hands you a note that the local papers have gotten word about a "strike in the penitentiary." Tell the press secretary that you have no comment on rumors; tell the department head to act vigorously to anticipate and prevent any disturbance. If a shakedown is necessary, by all means do a shakedown.

11:50 a.m.—You pick up the final outline of your speech for Rotary and your scheduling secretary walks to the car with you to explain the afternoon schedule.

12:10 p.m.—Arrive at Rotary where you greet about thirty or forty people, trying your best to remember all of the names, and then sit down between the president and the vice-president of the club to eat your lunch. At 12:50, as you are rapidly revising your notes, the head table is introduced and suddenly the governor is called upon to speak. Relying on a store of old jokes that you fear they have probably heard before (maybe even from you), you make your speech and call for questions and answers. Club adjourns at 1:30 and you head back to the office.

1:45 p.m.—Back in the office, you meet with your scheduling secretary to go over the lists of requests that have come in since yesterday (about twenty to thirty requests are received each day) and hear that one cabinet officer and one business leader "must" see you before the day is over.

2:00 p.m.—Meet with another cabinet officer and a local business leader to discuss the management and efficiency report on one of your departments. For a half an hour, you review in some detail the various recommendations of the business task force to make sure there has been follow through. At 2:30, after thanking the businessman for the incredible time and effort he has put in, you spend a private two minutes talking to the cabinet official about a particularly recalcitrant division head in his department.

2:30 p.m.—Meet with another cabinet official who is having trouble with her budget analyst and the Joint Budget Committee and devise a strategy as to how to make the JBC understand the nature of the problem. Promise to call the Chairman of the JBC and as the department head gathers up her papers to leave, ask your secretary to place the call.

3:00-3:30 p.m.—Has been reserved as "Governor's Time" on the schedule. Phone calls are returned, four more letters are signed and several new matters that have come up during the afternoon are reviewed. You dictate two letters, one concerning savings and loan regulations and the other a cover letter for an application for federal funds. A local businessman calls, asking you to call another state to encourage a business to locate a new plant in Colorado; while that call is being placed, you read a memo regarding the 3:30 meeting.

3:30 p.m.—A Department of Administration delegation comes in for its budget review, along with staff from your Office of State Planning and Budgeting. The meeting commences with a review of the computer plan of the state and a full discussion of whether to centralize or decentralize the computer system. Everybody recognizes, with sadness, that the state's computer system is six years or more behind that of private industry. You pull out a note from the day before from another department head that her offices are not being cleaned and give it to the head of the Department of Administration for follow-up. The department head asks for direction on how to handle a particular legislator who is seeking some politically charged information from the department and informs you he is also having some slight trouble with your legislative liaison. Before the meeting is over, your secretary buzzes on the intercom and reports that there are four aides waiting to see the governor and that there

174

is also a press emergency and the press secretary needs to see the governor "right away."

4:00 p.m.—Press secretary comes in with a report that one of the local newspapers is doing an article on how much money was expended in the last campaign. You tell the press secretary to call the former campaign director and get all the information the press needs and agree upon a quote that "campaigns have become outrageously expensive." Next, you turn, one at a time, to the other four aides who are waiting outside the door, each with a problem needing immediate attention. Three of the problems can be solved; on the fourth you ask for a memo by the end of the day.

4:10 p.m.—The head of Institutions calls to remind you that as head of the Human Resources Committee for the National Governors' Association, you have to make a speech in Chicago the following week and the department needs some direction to help prepare the speech.

4:30 p.m.—The chairman of the state Democratic (or Republican) party comes in to discuss a complaint about the governor's boards and commission appointments: the party "is not being listened to." You promise the party head that you will discuss the problem with staff but that the chairperson must recognize that appointments must be bipartisan and, in some cases, even nonpartisan. The press secretary comes back with another specific question on another story that is breaking about the penitentiary and you sit down and call the head of the Department of Corrections to get a late report on the pending disturbance.

4:55 p.m.—A group of school kids with a teacher who once worked on the governor's campaign ask if they can quickly peek in the office and the governor ushers them in and gives them three minutes on the history of the State Capitol.

5:00 p.m.—Security people come in to inform you that you are late for a ribbon cutting scheduled for five o'clock at a local downtown building and that the traffic is heavy. You leave immediately and use the car phone to return two of the calls that you didn't have a chance to return during the day.

While the calls are being placed, you go over the brief remarks for the ribbon cutting and at 5:05 p.m. arrive to find an impatient delegation waiting.

5:05-5:15 p.m.—Ribbon cutting followed by a quick round of handshaking with the officials of the new enterprise. Stop by one cocktail party honoring a new Canadian banking group, then home at 6:00 p.m. for the evening news.

6:00-6:30 p.m.—Watch the evening news while signing more letters. (At the end of every day, a full briefcase of files, memos, letters and letters to be signed follows the governor and has to be disposed of before the next evening.) You attempt to sign as much of your mail as possible while watching the six o'clock national news, interrupting it once for another call from the press secretary asking for one last quote about the story on campaign spending.

6:30-7:10 p.m.—Eat dinner with the family while trying to forget the prison disturbance, the story on campaign spending, and the myriad other issues dealt with during the day. Hear about your daughter's fourth-grade excursion to the museum and discuss family vacation plans for next summer.

7:10-7:20 p.m.—The kids leave the table. You discuss the mansion budget with your wife while finishing your coffee.

7:20-7:45 p.m.—Go upstairs, shower, change your suit, and look over your notes for your evening speech.

7:45 p.m.—Leave for the Brown Palace Hotel for an eight o'clock speech to the Food Retailers. Look in your notebook to remember the name of the doorman at the Brown Palace, say hello to the assistant manager who is there to greet you, and go to the second floor where the dinner is already in progress. Explain again to the dinner chairman you are sorry that you missed cocktails and dinner but that you try to limit invitations to permit you to have dinner with your family regularly. He, in turn, explains that the cocktail party ran overtime and the dinner is running a half an hour late. Sit down and try to avoid the temptation of having another dessert while you are waiting for the speech to begin.

8:35 p.m.—Introduction by the food retailers' president ("A governor who we haven't always agreed with but who has always taken the time to listen"). Give speech.

9:10 p.m.—Speech over, present a plaque to the food retailer of the year and have pictures taken with the officers of the organization.

9:30 p.m.—Leave the Brown Palace, get home, get into something more comfortable and sign more mail while watching the ten o'clock news.

10:30 p.m.—Lay down your pen on a stack of letters that need to be signed tomorrow morning because you are just too tired to finish them tonight.

10:35 p.m.—To bed.

It is clear that, while a governor might think that he has captured the governorship, the office in fact has captured him. The job, to a large degree, is reactive; there is a constant need to make choices—on policy, on time, on strategy. Realistically, but tragically, Colorado's governor is like all governors who find little time to pursue their broad strategies and instead spend a considerable amount of time responding to day-to-day pressures.

Essay on Sources

Colorado's governors have not attracted the attention of writers and historians. The significance of this oversight would be hard to determine. The search for information on these men, therefore, takes on the complexities of solving a historical mystery, involving plenty of hard work to uncover facts and insights into their characters. Curiously, despite a wealth of sources, the most difficult governors to "flesh out" are the most recent.

The best place to initiate the search is in general Colorado histories and their bibliographies. Carl Ubbelohde, Maxine Benson, and Duane A. Smith, *A Colorado History* (Pruett, 1982), Robert G. Athearn, *The Coloradans* (University of New Mexico, 1976), and Carl Abbott, Stephen Leonard, and David McComb, *Colorado* (Colorado Associated University Press, 1982) provide the most up-to-date starting points. For the nineteenth century, Frank Hall's multi-volume *History of the State of Colorado* (Blakely, 1890-1895) gives intriguing glimpses of most of the early governors, whom Hall knew personally. The *Colorado Magazine* contains a wealth of articles and comments, particularly on individual governors and Helen Cannon's series on first ladies.

Two older and still very useful volumes are R. G. Dill, *The Political Campaigns of Colorado* (Arapahoe Publishing, 1895) and Fitz-Mac (James MacCarthy), *Political Portraits* (Gazette Printing, 1888). Only two of the governors under discussion have received full-length biographies, Thomas L. Karnes, *William Gilpin: Western Nationalist* (University of Texas, 1970) and John Morris, *Davis H. Waite* (University Press, 1982).

There are a group of masters' theses that proved most helpful: see Majorie Hornbein, "Colorado's Amazing Gubernatorial Election Contest of 1904," (University of Denver, 1967); Lloyd K. Musselman, "Governor John F. Shafroth and the Colorado Progressives: Their Fight for Direct Legislation," (University of Denver, 1961); Harold E.

Rathgeber, "The Public Life of Alva Adams," (University of Denver, 1954); Robert C. Voight, "The Life of John Long Routt," (University of Northern Colorado, 1947); Gerald D. Welch, "John F. Shafroth, Progressive Governor of Colorado, 1910-1912," (University of Denver, 1962); M. Paul Holsinger, "Amache: The Story of Japanese Relocation in Colorado," (University of Denver, 1960), and Patrick McCarty, "Big Ed Johnson," (University of Colorado, 1958).

Newspapers convey a bonanza of contemporary opinions and counter-opinions, as well as editorial reactions and a chronology of events of all administrations. Of the men and politics included in this book, more references may be found to Davis Waite and the election of 1904 and its aftermath than any others. To place Colorado governors within the context of other state governors and the federal framework, see James MacGregor Burns, J.W. Peltason, and Thomas E. Cronin, *Government by the People* (Prentice-Hall, 1984).

For those interested in continuing the search further, it is now time to delve into original sources, including state and legislative publications. Once the researcher acquires a feel for the era and the man, the most important single source of records is the Colorado State Archives with its holdings of official documents and governors' papers. The next step would be a visit to the library of the Colorado Historical Society, the Western History Department of the Denver Public Library, and the Western Historical Collections, University of Colorado, which contain both secondary and primary materials. The challenges are many, the rewards infinite, not the least being exploration of that captivating world of Colorado's yesterday.

Appendix: Colorado's Territorial Governors

	Born and Died	Party	Term
William Gilpin	October 4, 1815- January 20, 1894	Republican	1861-62
John Evans	March 9, 1814- July 3, 1897	Republican	1862-65
Alexander Cummings	November 17, 1810- July 16, 1879	Republican	1865-67
A. Cameron Hunt	December 25, 1829- May 14, 1894	Republican	1867-69
Edward M. McCook	June 15, 1833- September 9, 1909	Republican	1869-73
Samuel H. Elbert	April 3, 1833- November 27, 1899	Republican	1873-74
Edward M. McCook	June 15, 1833- September 9, 1909	Republican	1874-75
John L. Routt	April 25, 1826- August 13, 1907	Republican	1875-77

Appendix:
Colorado's Governors

	Born and Died	Party	Term
John L. Routt	April 25, 1826- August 13,1907	Republican	1877-79
Frederick W. Pitkin	August 31,1837- December 18, 1886	Republican	1879-83
James B. Grant	January 2, 1848- November 7, 1911	Democrat	1883-85
Benjamin H. Eaton	December 15, 1833- October 29, 1904	Republican	1885-87
Alva Adams	May 14, 1850- November 1, 1922	Democrat	1887-89
Job A. Cooper	November 6, 1843- January 20, 1899	Republican	1889-91
John L. Routt	April 25, 1826- August 13, 1907	Republican	1891-93
Davis H. Waite	April 9, 1825- November 28, 1901	Populist	1893-95
Albert W. McIntire	January 15, 1853- January 30, 1935	Republican	1895-97
Alva Adams	May 14, 1850- November 1, 1922	Democrat	1897-99
Charles S. Thomas	December 6, 1849- June 24, 1934	Democrat	1899-1901
James B. Orman	November 4, 1849- July 21, 1919	Democrat	1901-03
James H. Peabody	August 21, 1852- November 23, 1917	Republican	1903-05
Alva Adams	May 14, 1850- November 1, 1922	Democrat	1905
James H. Peabody	August 21, 1852- November 23, 1917	Republican	1905
Jesse F. McDonald	June 30, 1858- February 25, 1941	Republican	1905-07
Henry A. Buchtel	September 30, 1847- October 22, 1924	Republican	1907-09

	Born and Died	Party	Ter
John F. Shafroth	June 8, 1854- February 20, 1922	Democrat	1909
Elias M. Ammons	July 28, 1860- May 20, 1925	Democrat	1913-
George A. Carlson	October 23, 1876- December 6, 1926	Republican	1915-
Julius C. Gunter	October 31, 1858- October 26, 1940	Democrat	1917-
Oliver H. Shoup	December 13, 1869- September 30, 1940	Republican	1919-
William E. Sweet	January 27, 1869- May 9, 1942	Democrat	1923-
Clarence J. Morley	December 9, 1869- November 15, 1948	Republican	1925-
William H. Adams	February 15, 1862- February 4, 1954	Democrat	1927-
Edwin C. Johnson	January 1, 1884- May 30, 1970	Democrat	1933-
Ray H. Talbot	August 19, 1896- January 30, 1955	Democrat	1937
Teller Ammons	December 3, 1895- January 16, 1972	Democrat	1937-
Ralph L. Carr	December 11, 1887- September 22, 1950	Republican	1939-4
John C. Vivian	June 30, 1887- February 10, 1954	Republican	1943-4
William L. Knous	February 2, 1889- December 12, 1959	Democrat	1947-5
Walter W. Johnson	April 16, 1904-	Democrat	1950-5
Daniel I.J. Thornton	January 31, 1911- January 18, 1976	Republican	1951-5
Edwin C. Johnson	January 1, 1884- May 30, 1970	Democrat	1955-5
Stephen L.R. McNichols	May 7, 1914-	Democrat	1957-6
John A. Love	November 29, 1916-	Republican	1963-7
John D. Vanderhoof	May 27, 1922-	Republican	1973-75
Richard D. Lamm	August 3, 1935-	Democrat	1975—

Index